The 3000 Questions About Myself Book

The 3000 Questions About Myself Book

A Thoughtfully Crafted Collection of Questions About Me for Adults of All Genders to Spark Deep Conversations, Self-Discovery, and Insight

Aria Capri Publishing Group
Mauricio Vasquez
Toronto, Canada

Authors:
Aria Capri Publishing Group
Mauricio Vasquez
First Printing: May 2025

ISBN 978-1-998729-43-2 (Electronic book)
ISBN 978-1-998729-42-5 (Hardcover book)
ISBN 978-1-998729-41-8 (Paperback)

Introduction

In every season of life, we pause—sometimes quietly, sometimes in chaos—and ask ourselves, *Who am I, really? What do I need? Where am I going?* These questions aren't signs of confusion; they're signals of growth. They're invitations to reconnect—with our values, our memories, our relationships, and the evolving stories we carry inside.

That's why this book exists.

The 3000 Questions About Myself Book is more than a collection of prompts—it's a companion for anyone seeking deeper clarity, emotional awareness, and more meaningful conversations. Whether you're on a path of personal transformation or simply curious to know yourself better, these thoughtfully crafted questions offer a space to pause, reflect, and reconnect with what truly matters.

As a writer and emotional intelligence coach, I've seen how powerful the *right question* can be. A well-timed prompt can unlock a memory long buried, shift a limiting belief, or open the door to a vulnerable, unforgettable conversation. This book was born from that belief—that self-discovery doesn't have to be complicated. It starts with one honest question. And then another.

With 3,000 questions covering everything from your everyday quirks to your deepest dreams, this book is designed to help you explore every corner of your inner world. It's a resource to return to again and again—alone or with others—whenever you're ready to dig a little deeper.

There's no single "right way" to move through these pages. Flip to any section that speaks to you. Read a few questions over coffee, explore them in your journal, or spark a soulful dinner conversation. Some prompts are lighthearted. Others go straight to the heart. All are here to help you learn more about yourself—and invite others to do the same.

You might use this book for:
- Solo reflection or meditation
- Group conversations, retreats, or coaching circles
- Intimate connection with a partner or friend
- Sparking self-awareness during life transitions
- Emotional check-ins and personal growth rituals

No matter how you engage, let the questions guide you—not toward perfect answers, but toward honest exploration.

In a world that rushes us toward certainty and fast answers, asking a slow, thoughtful question is a radical act. It centers your voice. It builds bridges between people. It helps you live more aligned with who you truly are.

Whether you're here to reconnect with yourself, deepen your relationships, or simply enjoy a more meaningful kind of conversation, you're in the right place.

So take a deep breath. Turn the page.

And let the journey begin—one question at a time.

How to Use This Book

- **Make a choice:** Each question invites you to pick a side or share a perspective—don't overthink it. The goal isn't perfection; it's reflection.

- **Go deeper:** Your first answer matters—but your why matters more. That's where the real insight and meaningful conversations begin.

- **Stay flexible:** There's no right way to move through this book. Start at the beginning or flip to a page that speaks to you. Reflect silently, journal your thoughts, or talk it out with someone you trust.

- **No wrong answers:** This space is judgment-free. Be honest. Be curious. Let yourself respond without filters.

- **Create space:** Silence the noise—phones off, distractions down. Give yourself or your group the gift of presence.

- **Wander freely:** If a question leads somewhere unexpected, follow it. The best discoveries often live off-script.

- **Enjoy the process:** Let these prompts spark laughter, insight, storytelling, or debate. Growth can be deep and lighthearted.

A Quick Favor to Ask

If this book has inspired reflection, sparked meaningful conversations, or brought you closer to someone in your life, I'd be incredibly grateful if you could take a moment to leave a review.

As an independent author without the resources of a big publishing house, your feedback truly makes a difference. Reviews help others discover this book, and they remind me why this work matters—one question, one reader at a time.

To share your thoughts, simply scan the QR code. It only takes a minute, but your words will go a long way.

Thank you, sincerely, for your time and support

Aria Capri Publishing

P.S. Don't miss your free bonus!

You'll find a special gift waiting for you at the **end of this book**—a digital version of *THIS IS MY WAY* you can download and keep with you wherever you go.

Loved This Book? You Might Also Enjoy...

  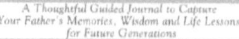 

The 3000 Questions About Myself

1. What's something you recently experienced that completely shifted how you see the world?

2. If someone offered you insight into your future, would you want to hear it? Why or why not?

3. Imagine you just earned a standing ovation at work — what do you hope it's for?

4. What recent question or curiosity led you to search online? What does that say about you?

5. When did you last take a full day to rest or recharge — pajamas included?

6. If you were a gemstone, which one would best represent your personality or inner strength?

7. What's a story about an animal doing something brave or inspiring that stayed with you?

8. If you could live in one season forever, which would you choose and why?

9. Describe a Monday that felt like complete chaos — and how you made it through.

10. If loyalty and truth came into conflict, how would you decide which matters more?

11. What single item in your home — if suddenly gone — would completely disrupt your daily life?

12. What's one important thing you keep delaying — and how would it feel to finally start it?

13. Have you ever tried to be funny but it went all wrong? What happened, and what did you learn?

14. What's one part of your daily routine you'd love to never have to do again?

15. What classic song from before your time feels like it was written just for you?

16. Is there a small superstition or quirky habit you still follow — even if you know it's silly?

17. If you could write three truths or hopes to share with strangers through fortune cookies, what would they say?

18. What two movies would become hilariously odd if their main characters swapped places?

19. What quality or trait do others consistently recognize in you — and how does that make you feel?

20. Do you think someone who commits a serious crime should spend their entire life in prison? Why or why not?

21. Which childhood TV character still makes you smile when you think about them? Why do they mean so much?

22. What's the strangest or most surprising historical fact you've ever come across — and why did it stick with you?

23. What's one small or meaningful thing you did today that you can feel good about?

24. If a bench was placed in your honor, where would it go — and what story would that place tell about you?

25. Imagine your online name turned into a scent — what kind of feeling or vibe would it give off?

26. If your face could inspire something powerful or meaningful, what would that be?

27. Which actor best captured the spirit of James Bond for you — charm, action, mystery, or wit?

28. What's one thing you've accomplished that others doubted — and how did it shape your story?

29. If you could rename a drinking glass, what creative or quirky name would you give it?

30. Looking back, what's one thing you would change if you could redo your high school years?

31. What's something you finally did after putting it off for a while — and how did it feel to get it done?

32. If you could share a microphone with anyone in the world, who would it be and what song would you choose together?

33. Is there someone from your past you still think about and wish you could reach out to? Why them?

34. What three personal care items make you feel most like yourself — grounded, expressive, or confident?

35. If your personality had a color palette, which three shades would you choose and why?

36. If animals had voices, which ones do you think would grumble the most — and what would they say?

37. Which Halloween treat do you secretly (or not-so-secretly) hope ends up in your candy stash every year?

38. If "dad jokes" are goofy and punny, what kind of joke do you think moms would be famous for?

39. How handy are you with practical skills like tying knots, changing a tire, or basic survival tasks?

40. If you could give a tail to an animal that doesn't have one, which would be the funniest or most surprising?

41. What's a moment when you felt totally awkward or exposed — but can laugh about now?

42. How do you usually respond when someone unexpected calls to sell you something?

43. If you had the chance to pick a brand-new name for yourself, what would it be and why?

44. What do you remember most about the last time you were in the ocean — the sights, the feeling, or the moment?

45. Which profession do you think has the most iconic or stylish uniform — and why does it stand out to you?

46. Has a random moment or meeting ever led to something big in your life? What changed because of it?

47. What's the most embarrassing or unexpected thing you've realized was stuck in your teeth?

48. Imagine finding a box of puppies outside your home — what's your next move?

49. What word do you wish people would stop using — one that feels hurtful, overused, or meaningless?

50. When it's your turn at karaoke, what's the song you belt out with heart and pride?

51. If protecting your child's feelings meant telling a small lie, how would you handle it?

52. What are your thoughts on intelligent life beyond Earth — curiosity, hope, or skepticism?

53. Who from your early years has remained in your life — and what has that bond taught you?

54. What idea or belief you once held as a child do you miss — and what did it give you?

55. If you could offer any gift — tangible or symbolic — to a newborn baby, what would it be and why?

56. In your eyes, what qualities — beyond IQ — truly define a genius?

57. Picture a surprise leak in your home — what's the first thing you'd instinctively reach for?

58. If distance wasn't an obstacle, where would you teleport right now — and what's drawing you there?

59. Can you invent a new, playful way of saying "for a really long time"?

60. Have you ever tried working out to a video or online class? What stuck with you about it?

61. If you had to rename the fly, what fun, odd, or fitting name would you give it?

62. When's the last time you got a tiny zap — and what were you doing just before it happened?

63. Before we had instant answers online, how did you search for things you wanted to learn or understand?

64. Which loud or jarring sounds tend to bother your senses the most — and how do you handle them?

65. If you could redesign your daily view, what would you want to see outside your window?

66. If you could add three new creatures to an animal cracker box, which ones would you choose and why?

67. If you had the chance to review a restaurant as a food critic, where would your first visit be and why?

68. Which font style feels most "you" — whether it's clean, playful, strong, or classic?

69. Have you ever let loose and slid down a bannister? What was the moment like?

70. Look around — how many balloons do you think could fit in this space if you filled it to the brim?

71. If money wasn't an issue for just one joyful purchase today, what would you treat yourself to?

72. When did you last dip your toes into something — water, sand, or even a new experience?

73. Can you remember the last time you took a social leap and talked to someone you didn't know?

74. If someone made a film about your life, who would best capture your story — and what would their vision be?

75. What film do people seem to love, but you just don't connect with — and why?

76. Is there a keychain you've held onto because it holds a memory, meaning, or moment?

77. Who do you think is the most instantly recognizable athlete in the world today or in history?

78. If you could revisit one single day from your past — to feel, enjoy, or understand it again — which would you choose?

79. Has there been a time when you were caught in a lie — and what did it teach you?

80. Can you remember the last time you saw a rainbow — and how did it make you feel in that moment?

81. If snowstorms are whiteouts, what creative name would you give to a rainstorm — and why?

82. What item or object in your life holds deep personal value — something you'd never want to lose?

83. What costume have you worn that made you feel the most creative, confident, or free?

84. If you were a witch living today, what would your modern tools or magical companions look like?

85. If losing a part of yourself meant gaining lifelong health, would you do it — or is the cost too high?

86. When you play Monopoly, what's your favorite property to go for — and is it strategy, nostalgia, or luck?

87. If someone handed you money to invest with no strings attached, where would you put it and why?

88. What's something you bought online — maybe from eBay — that turned out to be an unexpectedly great find?

89. What's the most creative or surprising way people use to communicate when words aren't available?

90. If you had an entire day to yourself with no responsibilities, where would you go and how would you spend it?

91. If you could have a conversation with any animal, which would you choose — and what would you want to know?

92. What factors would guide your decision if a beloved pet's suffering made euthanasia a heartbreaking consideration?

93. What place name do you think would sound hilarious or surprising if a celebrity gave it to their baby?

94. Where would you want to sit on a long flight — window, aisle, front, back — and what makes that your perfect spot?

95. What's the most ridiculous, fun, or competitive thing you've ever raced against the clock to accomplish?

96. You're in public with a runny nose and no tissue — how do you handle the awkwardness?

97. Which fairground ride makes you feel the most joy, freedom, or nostalgia — and what keeps you coming back?

98. You're stranded with no direct route and little gas — how do you get creative and stay calm?

99. What's the longest book you've made it through — and what kept you turning the pages?

100. If you lived as a modern genie, where would you hide — and how would someone call on your magic?

101. If you had to sum up your closest friend in just one word, what would it be — and why?

102. How do you feel about cities removing cars from downtown areas to make room for people instead?

103. Can you recall a recent moment when something could've gone wrong — but you narrowly escaped it?

104. Have you ever acted like you weren't home to avoid a visitor — and who was it that made you hide?

105. If you had to swap your hands for something strange but useful, what would you choose and why?

106. What objects, places, or feelings do you associate with your favorite color — and why?

107. If someone offered you money for a selfie, would you agree — or question their motives?

108. What truth — though painful — helped you grow or see life differently?

109. When did you last have a real chat with someone living nearby — and do you know their names?

110. Has a teacher ever underestimated you — and did you prove them wrong later on?

111. What activity is considered a sport, but in your opinion, doesn't really qualify — and why?

112. If you suddenly had a free afternoon, how would you spend it — rest, joy, or adventure?

113. Have you ever taken a bite or sip of something thinking it was one thing — only to be very surprised?

114. Which actor seems to live the same way off-screen as the characters they play on-screen?

115. In your eyes, what traits, choices, or impact make a person legendary?

116. When it comes to trivia or fun facts, what topic always gives you confidence?

117. If you had a second chance at education, would you choose to go to college — or do something different?

118. Have you ever heard of a tattoo fail that made you laugh or cringe — what was the spelling mistake?

119. If you could only move forward in life — literally — how would that shift your habits or decisions?

120. Can you recall a moment when your body betrayed you in public — and how did you recover from it?

121. If you could design your sibling lineup, would you want brothers, sisters, both — or none at all?

122. If you could extend your pet's life by giving up a year of your own, would you make that trade?

123. What's the most unexpected or funny sound you've ever heard a bird copy?

124. If you had to guess — or test — how many gummy bears you could fit in your mouth, what would your number be?

125. If your schedule allowed, which cause or organization would you love to support with your time — and why?

126. What's your favorite humorous or gentle phrase to describe someone who might not be the quickest thinker?

127. Do you ever peek at someone's profile to understand them better — and who's the last person you looked up?

128. What's the largest or most vulnerable favor you've ever requested — and how did that feel?

129. Besides relatives, have you ever met someone with your same last name — and did it feel like a connection?

130. If a lost dog followed you home, how would you respond — with compassion, caution, or curiosity?

131. As your day ends, what three moments — big or small — are you most thankful for?

132. If your job interviewer didn't show up, how would you react — wait, leave, follow up, or adapt?

133. What's a playful, harmless prank you've pulled that still makes you laugh to remember?

134. If you had one minute to choose a free trip anywhere in the world, where would your heart take you?

135. If you could choose a version of yourself that feels healthiest and happiest, what would that look like?

136. Which Sesame Street character captured your heart — and what did they teach or represent for you?

137. Is there someone in your life — playful or serious — who feels like your opposite or rival?

138. Can you remember the last time you shared a smile with a stranger — and how it made you (or them) feel?

139. Thinking back, which decade — whether you lived it or admire it — feels the most exciting or meaningful to you?

140. If your day had a soundtrack, what type of music — or specific song — would fit the mood?

141. How many couples do you know who fell in love young and made it all the way through life together?

142. Is there a certain food you love — or avoid — because it always leads to indigestion or discomfort?

143. Have you ever rolled dice and stepped into a fantasy world by playing Dungeons and Dragons (or something similar)?

144. When did you last realize you made a small problem feel much bigger than it actually was?

145. What do you think would surprise or disappoint a visitor from 50 years ago about today's world?

146. In what moments do you seek solitude — and what does it give you emotionally or mentally?

147. Can you think of a trend, product, or idea that was wildly popular — but didn't live up to the hype?

148. How would you honestly rate your current eating habits — from a scale of 1 (yikes) to 10 (thriving)?

149. After Generations X, Y, and Z, what creative name would you give the next generation?

150. If your time had a price, how many years would you be willing to exchange for a huge sum of money — if any?

151. If you were stuck on an island, which six people — famous, friends, or fictional — would you want with you?

152. Have you ever gotten into a place — an event, a movie, a party — without paying for it? What happened?

153. If you had to show aliens what Earth is all about in just a few stops, where would you take them first?

154. Can you list some famous singing pairs where a male and female artist teamed up for unforgettable songs?

155. What unusual or surprising foods do you secretly think would taste amazing covered in chocolate?

156. As a cartoon character immune to harm, how would you land after falling from an airplane — with style, drama, or silliness?

157. What's your favorite funny or dramatic way to describe extreme tiredness?

158. In today's world, would you ever pick up a hitchhiker? Why or why not?

159. If you could choose a spirit animal that reflects your inner self, what would it be — and why?

160. If you could instantly change your height, would you go taller, shorter, or stay just as you are?

161. Are you a creature of habit when shopping, following the same supermarket route each time?

162. Looking back, what childhood award — big or small — made you feel most proud?

163. If people spoke about you a century from now, what story or quality would you want them to remember?

164. In your opinion, who in the world of sports has crossed the line the worst?

165. Which actor would make audiences laugh — or groan — if they were cast as Indiana Jones?

166. If you were on a quiz show and had to choose a specialty, what topic would you totally ace?

167. In your view, what makes someone proudly or lovingly a "nerd"?

168. Have you ever arrived at a hotel expecting luxury, only to find... a very different story?

169. If you caught a coworker stealing, how would you handle the situation — quietly, confrontationally, or formally?

170. Can you remember the last time you shared a bath — and what made that moment special or funny?

171. In what situations do you believe playing it safe is absolutely the right choice?

172. If you had to shout a word in a crowd that would cause immediate reaction, what would it be?

173. What dreams, hopes, or rewards are waiting for you when your metaphorical "ship" arrives?

174. What's the final habit, thought, or ritual you do before closing your eyes at night?

175. If you won a dream cruise for two, who would you invite to share the journey and why?

176. Imagine: if everyone on Earth jumped at once, what crazy or surprising thing do you think would happen?

177. When you look at your TV remote, do you really know what all those buttons actually do?

178. If you could invent a creative or funny name for your favorite shade of beige, what would it be?

179. If there were a new, modern "Fifth Musketeer," what creative name would you give them?

180. Can you remember the last time you shared a bath — and what made that moment special or funny?

181. In what situations do you believe playing it safe is absolutely the right choice?

182. If you had to shout a word in a crowd that would cause immediate reaction, what would it be?

183. What dreams, hopes, or rewards are waiting for you when your metaphorical "ship" arrives?

184. What's the final habit, thought, or ritual you do before closing your eyes at night?

185. If you won a dream cruise for two, who would you invite to share the journey and why?

186. Imagine: if everyone on Earth jumped at once, what crazy or surprising thing do you think would happen?

187. When you look at your TV remote, do you really know what all those buttons actually do?

188. If you could invent a creative or funny name for your favorite shade of beige, what would it be?

189. If there were a new, modern "Fifth Musketeer," what creative name would you give them?

190. Do you think breakdancing deserves a place alongside traditional Olympic events — why or why not?

191. What's the oddest or funniest scientific name you've ever heard for an animal, plant, or anything else?

192. What situation made you laugh (or worry) about your own sanity recently?

193. What "most likely to..." awards would you give three of your friends, based on who they are?

194. What's one subject, skill, or area of life you wish you knew more about?

195. Have you ever had a funny, awkward, or downright awful experience in a changing room?

196. If you could harmlessly haunt someone just for laughs, who would you choose and why?

197. What's something in your life you know deserves more of your attention — but often gets overlooked?

198. If you could dream up what's happening inside Area 51 in a parallel universe, what would it be?

199. Would you ever part with your hair for a good cause — and how would that make you feel?

200. Are you superstitious about things like walking under ladders, or do you see it as just a silly myth?

201. Can you remember the most intense storm you experienced — and what feelings or memories does it bring back?

202. When packing the perfect picnic, what three foods do you absolutely have to bring along?

203. If money weren't an issue, would you stay in your current field — or chase a passion instead?

204. What's the most unexpected or silly way you've ever gotten hurt — and does it still make you laugh?

205. Have you ever been brave — or grossed out — enough to help someone else with a pimple emergency?

206. Can you remember the last time you let out a real, full-on scream — and what caused it?

207. If you created an immortal character, what ordinary object would be their secret weakness?

208. What's one job, chore, or challenge you would really dread doing completely alone?

209. Have you ever explored a national park — and which ones left the biggest impression on you?

210. When it comes to protecting your digital life, what's your go-to backup method and why?

211. If Alice visited a different Wonderland, what new characters — strange, wild, or wonderful — might she meet?

212. Can you remember a moment when you suddenly realized, "I'm really an adult now"? What were you doing?

213. If you could add anything to your car — for fun, comfort, or adventure — what would it be?

214. Do you think every worker, no matter how good, can eventually be replaced — or do some people feel irreplaceable?

215. If you were home alone, what sound would immediately make you feel uneasy or afraid?

216. Have you ever camped out or bundled up in a sleeping bag — and where was it?

217. Are there certain smells that instantly make you feel nauseous — even if they're common for others?

218. If you had to be a giant gnome statue in a garden forever, what funny or powerful pose would you strike?

219. Which Scooby-Doo gang member do you feel you're most like — and what traits make you say that?

220. If your friends had to rate your dance skills out of 10, what score do you think they would give you?

221. Out of all your Facebook friends, how many do you actually see and spend real time with these days?

222. What's the one thing you always keep with you, just in case something unexpected happens?

223. If you suddenly became the main character from the last TV show you watched, who would you be — and how would you feel about it?

224. Which Disney movie holds a special place in your heart — and if none do, what draws you away from them?

225. If you were asked to lead any group, cause, or team, what would you want to be in charge of?

226. If you use non-dairy milk, which one do you like best — and what do you love about it?

227. If you could only have one pie on Thanksgiving — sweet or savory — what would you pick?

228. After laptops and palmtops, what portable tech device do you think should be invented next?

229. In your heart, do you believe it's truly possible to forgive someone — and actually forget the hurt?

230. If the world became one nation, which city would make the best capital for everyone — and why?

231. What's the toughest physical task you've ever had to do — and what did you learn from it?

232. Would you be willing to try squirrel meat if you had the chance — or have you already?

233. If given the choice, would you take a luxury car worth more or a smaller pile of cash to spend your way?

234. On average, how many hours do you spend each week watching TV or streaming shows?

235. Have you ever worn a traditional outfit from another culture — and what was the experience like?

236. If your best friend got three wishes today, what would they probably wish for first?

237. If you had to pack the highest-calorie, energy-rich food for a two-day hike, what would you choose?

238. How much would someone have to offer you to put on — and keep — 100 extra pounds for an entire year?

239. Is there a herb or spice you consistently skip in recipes — and what's your reason for leaving it out?

240. What's the tiniest or grossest thing you've accidentally sat on — and what was your reaction?

241. If you had to visit wherever your blindfolded pin landed, what place would you secretly hope to avoid?

242. What's the latest new word you added to your vocabulary — and how did you come across it?

243. If you created a coat of arms for your family, what symbols would you choose to represent who you are?

244. What's the coolest, most awe-inspiring moment you've ever watched in slow motion?

245. What actor do you think always gets stuck playing the same type of character?

246. In your opinion, what combination of food, drink, and setting creates the perfect breakfast?

247. If you had to transform into any insect, which would you choose — and what makes it fit your personality?

248. If you ended up in an ER suddenly, what outfit would be the most embarrassing to show up in?

249. How many people, brands, or groups do you follow on social media — and does that number surprise you?

250. If you could invent a brand-new flavor of cotton candy, what delicious idea would you bring to life?

251. When did you last hop on a seesaw — and what memories or feelings did it bring back?

252. What's a cultural tradition from around the world that you found wonderfully strange or fascinating?

253. If a blackout hit your home and neighborhood tonight, what would be your first move?

254. Are there times when you accept second best — and when do you insist on only the best?

255. What three ingredients are your secret to blending the perfect, delicious smoothie?

256. Besides KFC, what's a meal or snack you think deserves the title of "finger lickin' good"?

257. If you could attend any music festival in the world, which one would you choose — and why?

258. If you could invent a brand-new dive, what would it look like — and what cool name would you give it?

259. Which science fiction movie do you believe offers the most realistic glimpse into Earth's possible future?

260. What current gadget would you love to see reimagined with gears, brass, and a steampunk twist?

261. Who was the last person you tossed a frisbee with, and where were you playing?

262. What's your go-to cookie when you're reaching for a glass of cold milk to go with it?

263. If today's thoughts scrolled above your head like a screen, how much explaining would you have to do?

264. What childhood story does your family love to tell — even if it still makes you blush a little?

265. Can you describe a time when the silence around you felt overwhelming or strangely loud?

266. Before heading off for a few days, what's the final thing you always make sure to do at home?

267. If you could reschedule your birthday to another day, what date would you pick — and why?

268. Is there a childhood toy you've held onto over the years — and what makes it special to you?

269. If you had to pull a MacGyver move and escape a flooded tunnel, what random things would you use to survive?

270. What's the funniest or most unfortunate name combination you've ever come across?

271. If you found food slightly past its expiration date, would you risk it — or toss it without hesitation?

272. If you spilled red wine on a white carpet, what would your first instinct be — panic, clean, or cover up?

273. If you could create your own magic word to cast a spell, what word would you choose — and why?

274. If you could create a new crazy movie like "Snakes on a Plane," what would you put on the plane instead?

275. Imagine your last meal turned into an art piece — what creative or funny title would you give it?

276. Have you ever spotted a face hidden in an object — and did it remind you of someone famous?

277. If you modernized Scooby-Doo's gang, what updated names would you give Velma, Daphne, and Fred?

278. When you were young, did the tooth fairy ever sneak into your room — and what did she leave behind?

279. What surprising or extraordinary event has happened in your life that you once thought was impossible?

280. Can you recall the last time you simply sat in total silence — and how did it make you feel?

281. If Alvin had a different name, what would you pick — and why would it suit him?

282. If you had to give up one sense for just 24 hours, which one would you pick — and why?

283. When you need solo entertainment, what one-player game do you love turning to?

284. Be honest: have you ever peeked inside someone's journal — and how did it make you feel afterward?

285. What's the last photo you captured that wasn't a selfie — and what inspired you to take it?

286. If you could instantly master any skill or talent, what would you choose — and why?

287. Have you ever swung at a piñata — and what's your funniest or most chaotic piñata memory?

288. Do you think Christmas decorations and songs should wait until December — or do you love an early start?

289. What's a task or chore you frustratingly keep forgetting, no matter how hard you try to remember?

290. On a typical day, how many hugs do you give — and how do they shape your day?

291. If you could rename the orange fruit without using the word "orange," what creative name would you pick?

292. Do you enjoy iced drinks like coffee or tea even when it's freezing outside — or do you switch to warm?

293. Which Clint Eastwood film sticks with you the most — or do his movies just not click for you?

294. If you could paint any landscape in the world, what view or place would you love to capture on canvas?

295. What's the coolest or most impressive thing you've seen someone do using their feet instead of their hands?

296. Which room at home feels like your "hub" — the place you naturally spend the most time?

297. If you could make one day show up only once every four years, like Leap Day, which would you choose?

298. If you could create the ultimate concert with three performers, living or gone, who would you bring together?

299. If you could earn a PhD based on your current knowledge, what subject would you suddenly be a doctor of?

300. What's a food that looks absolutely delicious but seriously disappointed your taste buds?

301. Have you ever passed off a store-bought cake as something you baked yourself?

302. If you could bring back the idea of "on a rope," what funny or useful thing would you create today?

303. What's your go-to facial expression that says everything without needing a single word?

304. If the letters in your name stood for something, what fun or meaningful words would they represent?

305. Where do you think would be the absolute worst place to experience a medical emergency like a heart attack?

306. When you think of holidays, what color pops into your mind first — and why?

307. Have you ever found yourself stocking up on food or supplies just in case things ran out?

308. If pandas could come in different colors instead of just black and white, what colors would you love to see?

309. If you could build something huge enough to be seen from space, what amazing thing would you make?

310. What food do you believe should always be eaten fresh for the best taste and experience?

311. Do you truly believe that anything is possible — or do you think some limits are just real?

312. If someone dared you, would you eat a beetle — or would you draw the line there?

313. If Hansel and Gretel lived today, what modern item would they use to leave a trail instead of breadcrumbs?

314. In your opinion, what combination of ice cream and soda makes the ultimate float?

315. Can you recall a time when your heart truly broke — and what helped you heal?

316. What habit, whether yours or someone else's, drives you absolutely crazy?

317. When did life last hit you with a moment that made you sigh, "Why me?" — and what caused it?

318. If you had just 30 seconds to say the alphabet backward under pressure, could you pull it off?

319. If you needed to make up a funny excuse for being late, what would your most creative one be?

320. Do you believe long-distance relationships can truly succeed — and what makes them last?

321. If plates were edible, what delicious flavor would you want them to have?

322. If you forgot your lunch today, what would you do — improvise, order in, or make a run for food?

323. What color do you think has fallen out of style — and are you still boldly wearing it?

324. Besides lemonade, what's the tastiest or most creative thing you love making with lemons?

325. Which Christmas carol gets stuck in your head — and not in a good way?

326. If you had to represent your country tomorrow in a sport, which one would you choose — even if you're not a pro?

327. What's something you used to argue passionately about — that now feels totally unimportant?

328. When it comes to ravioli, what filling wins your heart every time?

329. What sound immediately makes you feel like summer is here — even before you see it?

330. Can you recall a small act of kindness that left a huge mark on your heart or life?

331. What's the most recent thing you asked your smart speaker — and did it help, surprise, or amuse you?

332. When you visit a farmers market, what are your must-buy items that make the trip special?

333. What do you think is the perfect first job for a teenager to learn responsibility and confidence?

334. How would you sum up your day so far using just three words?

335. If you could "wallow" in something just for fun or comfort, what would you happily roll around in?

336. If a TV network called wanting to interview you about your company, what's your first move?

337. What's something clever or beautiful you could create if all you had was a stack of old newspapers?

338. When life gets tough, who's your go-to person for help, advice, or a listening ear?

339. If one ancient monument disappeared forever, which one would break your heart to lose?

340. If you could be a news anchor for one day, what exciting story would you want to announce live?

341. How would you rewrite the ending of Little Red Riding Hood to surprise or inspire readers?

342. Do you believe angels exist — and have you ever had an experience that felt like you met one?

343. If you had to make a "leftovers pie," what terrible ingredients would turn it into a disaster?

344. If your friends made up a nickname based on your vibe or attitude, what do you think it would be?

345. If you could own any famous movie prop, what iconic item would you love to have?

346. Have you ever eaten so much that you just had to lie down afterward — and when did it happen?

347. What are three things, big or small, that you're feeling cheerful or grateful for right now?

348. How many people in your life share your first name — and do you like having that name in common?

349. Can you remember the last time something made you light up and say, "That's cool!" — what was it?

350. If you could bring any mythical creature to life, which one would you choose and why?

351. If visitors asked you for the best place to eat in your town, where would you proudly send them?

352. Would you try mysterious food without asking what it is — and have you ever taken that brave leap?

353. What's the weirdest or most unbelievable cult you've ever learned about?

354. If you had to show you were angry without saying a word, how would you express it physically?

355. Are the clocks in your home set to a 24-hour format — or do you prefer the classic 12-hour style?

356. Have you ever found yourself struggling with something that was supposed to be "idiot-proof"?

357. When it comes to cake, what's your absolute favorite type of frosting?

358. When was the last time you really let loose and had a blast — a night that deserves its own theme year?

359. What's the tiniest, most delicate thing you've ever noticed out in nature?

360. If you invented the strongest adhesive ever, what creative name would you give it?

361. In a parallel world, what funny or epic new names would Butch Cassidy and the Sundance Kid have?

362. If you could magically finish any household chore by flipping a switch, which one would you pick first?

363. Which scents instantly calm or soothe you — reminding you to slow down and breathe?

364. Imagine a movie based on the number of weddings and funerals you've attended — what's the title?

365. Which children's story character gave you chills or nightmares when you were little?

366. If the "Twelve Days of Christmas" was written today, what modern gifts would you include?

367. Which radio station — or streaming channel — do you tune into the most for news, music, or talk shows?

368. Have you (or someone you know) ever come up with funny or innocent nicknames for private body parts?

369. If the wind stole your umbrella, how far or how long would you actually run after it?

370. In your opinion, how many fries would be a fair swap for one chicken nugget?

371. Which celebrity do you think has aged gracefully and looks even better today than in their youth?

372. If baboons didn't have blue bottoms, what fun or wild color would you give them instead?

373. Have you ever battled with "easy open" packaging — and how did that go?

374. What's the last thing that made you itch uncontrollably — an insect bite, fabric, or mystery itch?

375. If you made a top ten pie list, which delicious pie would grab your number one spot?

376. In your view, what key elements make a wedding outfit stand out as stylish and unforgettable?

377. Do you think there's someone out there who looks just like you — and have you ever met your "twin"?

378. Besides "thingamajig," what funny or creative words do you use when you can't remember the real name?

379. Do you think ancient human remains in museums should be respectfully returned to their original homeland?

380. If bubble gum came in savory flavors, what unique or delicious flavor would you want to try?

381. Have you ever seen a gravestone that truly touched your heart or made you feel deeply sad?

382. When's the last time something bad happened and you couldn't help but say, "That sucks!"?

383. What's the most unusual or surprising sport or game you've ever played?

384. If you could only keep three pictures from your phone, which ones would you save and why?

385. What three songs turn into your private concert when you're singing in the shower?

386. Are you a podcast listener — and what's the latest episode or series you tuned into?

387. When you need to power through a task, what songs do you crank up to get it done?

388. Do you see yourself as someone who works hard — and what goal or project are you focusing on today?

389. What's your favorite Bruce Springsteen song — or why hasn't his music made your playlist?

390. If you captained a pirate ship, what bold or clever name would you choose for it?

391. Looking back, what school subject do you find you've used the most in real life?

392. Besides money, what would you love to see growing on trees that could make life sweeter?

393. Where do you think getting a painful boil would be the most uncomfortable or annoying?

394. What's the weirdest or most unexpected fear (phobia) you've ever heard someone have?

395. If Buddy Holly had lived longer, what do you think his next great song would have been called?

396. What's one piece of advice from your parents you once ignored but now realize was spot-on?

397. If you could have an endless supply of just one candy forever, which delicious treat would you pick?

398. What's the absolute worst disaster that could happen mid-toothbrush?

399. If you could instantly earn a new degree, license, or certification, what would you want to have?

400. Was there a time in your life when you wished you were older — and why?

401. Is there a car color you just can't stand — and why does it rub you the wrong way?

402. If you created a revolutionary new energy source, what would it be made from — and what cool name would it have?

403. What's a silly or unexpected thing that made you tear up recently — even if it caught you off guard?

404. If you woke up after a hundred-year nap, what big changes in the world would shock you the most?

405. The last time you flipped a coin, what two options were you trying to decide between?

406. Have you ever reached halfway through a book and thought, "Nope, not finishing this one"?

407. What popular movie do you think deserves a new, better, or funnier title — and what would it be?

408. If your friends lost you in a bookstore, which section would they find you browsing in first?

409. After a breakup, what's the one thing you definitely do NOT want to hear from anyone?

410. In your opinion, which animal holds the title for being the most dangerous — and why?

411. If you could create your own theme park, what would it be about and who would it be for?

412. If cartoon characters could rap, which one would have the best flow and attitude?

413. Imagine Earth 10,000 years from today — what do you think the world will look like?

414. Is there a type of person or behavior you find hard to sympathize with — even when you try?

415. Have you ever "cleaned" a room quickly by shoving everything into a closet and hoping it stayed closed?

416. When did you last feel so confident and fired up that you thought, "Bring it on!" — and what was happening?

417. If you could paint a hidden funny message on the bottom of your boat, what would it say?

418. If you could invent your own twist on Monopoly, what fun or wild theme would you use?

419. Have you ever regretted buying something shortly after — and what was the item that made you sigh?

420. If you could imagine the worst idea for a drive-thru service, what would it be?

421. If you could fill a shopping cart with free food and drinks today, what would be your top picks?

422. What's the weirdest or most creative object you've ever used to hold your place in a book?

423. Can you remember the last time you put yourself first — even if just a little — and what happened?

424. Have you ever heard a funny real-life example where a person's name matched their profession perfectly?

425. When you chew gum, which brand do you like best — and what makes it your favorite?

426. If your personality could be captured by a salad dressing, what flavor would fit you best?

427. What's the most recent thing — big or small — that made you laugh so hard you couldn't help yourself?

428. Is there a piece of jewelry you always wear — something meaningful, stylish, or comforting?

429. What's a "buy one, get one free" deal that would be completely useless to you?

430. If you had to rate the embarrassment level of your passport photo from 1 to 10, what would you give it?

431. What's the strangest, funniest, or most unexpected thing you've ever spotted in a museum?

432. Would your dance moves get wilder or sillier if you knew no one could see you?

433. If cats came in every color, would you pick one to match your furniture — or go for something wild?

434. If you were stuck with a non-flushing toilet in someone else's house, what would your plan be?

435. Have you ever roasted marshmallows over a fire — and when was the last cozy or messy time you did it?

436. If you were creating the Olympic mascot for your hometown, what fun character would you design?

437. If a makeover team invaded your room, what color combo would make you cringe the most?

438. If you could relive your teenage years in any decade, which era would you pick and why?

439. If you got to join the Power Rangers, what color suit would you proudly wear?

440. Without looking it up, how many European capital cities can you name off the top of your head?

441. If you had to pick a pop princess to lead a heavy metal band, who would be the funniest choice?

442. If you could take lessons in anything — serious, fun, or totally random — what would you choose?

443. If your personality could be described as a scent, what would it smell like — fresh, spicy, sweet, bold?

444. Looking back, what's one cringe-worthy teenage moment you still shake your head about?

445. If you created a brand-new board game, what creative or funny playing pieces would you design?

446. Which three songs have stuck around on your playlists longer than any others — and why?

447. Besides playing the game, what creative or funny uses could you find for a ping-pong ball?

448. If you recast Charlie's Angels with all men, which three actors would you choose for a fresh twist?

449. In your heart, what's the true difference between simply existing and truly living?

450. Have you ever had that strange feeling like you've lived a moment before — and what was it like?

451. If you and your friends formed a bowling team, what hilarious or cool name would you pick?

452. If cobwebs were rainbow-colored or glittery, would you still sweep them away or admire them?

453. What's the oldest natural wonder — like an ancient tree, fossil, or canyon — that you've witnessed?

454. Can you recall a time when you smiled and stayed strong even though you were hurting inside?

455. Where were you shopping when someone really impressed you with great service — and what were you buying?

456. If you could score free season tickets to any team's games, which sport and team would you choose?

457. Which board game do you always love playing — and what makes it your favorite?

458. When you set New Year's resolutions, do you usually stick to them — or do they fade by February?

459. Would you ever choose to be frozen with the hope of waking up in a future world?

460. How many people in your life — friends, family, colleagues — have names starting with B?

461. What's the best deal or steal you ever scored during a sale?

462. If cockroaches could talk, what would their voices sound like — and what would they grumble about?

463. Where have you witnessed the absolute worst parking job — and what made it unforgettable?

464. If you had to pick just one kind of bread forever, what loaf or roll would win your heart?

465. What's the easiest or fastest way you've ever earned money — and how did it happen?

466. If you had a live mic right now to give a radio shout-out, who would you send love or thanks to?

467. What's the weirdest or most unusual room you've ever entered — and what brought you there?

468. Do you believe animals deserve the same basic rights as people — and why or why not?

469. If The Wizard of Oz was set today, what modern twist would Dorothy's magic shoes have?

470. What's the most recent thing that truly made you stop and say, "Wow!" out loud?

471. If you could safely visit any planet in our solar system, which one would you choose and why?

472. What's the weirdest or most surprising item living in the trunk of your car right now?

473. Have you ever competed in a burping contest — and were you victorious or hilariously defeated?

474. What's the coolest or most mind-bending optical illusion you've ever seen — and how did it trick you?

475. If dinosaurs lived today, where do you think they would thrive — deserts, jungles, oceans?

476. Do you remember singing "Frère Jacques" as a kid — and can you still hum or sing the words?

477. When you play trivia, what quiz category usually trips you up — history, sports, geography, or something else?

478. If someone leaves you hanging on a high-five, how do you play it off coolly or make a joke of it?

479. Have you ever thought someone was lying only to find out they were telling the truth — and what happened?

480. If black holes could be a different color, what shade would make them feel less scary and more welcoming?

481. How many gadgets in your home regularly beep, buzz, or chirp for your attention?

482. What's one habit you have that you feel wastes resources — and are you trying to change it?

483. If your week so far were turned into a dance, what style would it be — wild, slow, or chaotic?

484. Which app on your phone is your daily lifesaver — and which one is useless but too fun to delete?

485. If you wanted to rule the world, what's the first clever or sneaky thing you would do?

486. If you could invent the most useless superhero ability ever, what would it be?

487. If you could invent a new fastener better than Velcro, what fun or crazy invention would it be?

488. What's your favorite ABBA song — and can you proudly sing every word, or do you fake a few?

489. When was the last time you ate alphabet pasta — and did you make any funny or clever words with it?

490. If you had ten golden tickets to anything — concert, event, adventure — what would you choose and who would you invite?

491. What three must-have features would make your dream treehouse a perfect place to hang out?

492. Have you ever waited forever in a line just to get something you really wanted — and was it worth it?

493. When was your last oops moment — pushing a door that very clearly said "pull"?

494. What hidden gem of a website have you found that you think more people should know about?

495. If you could magically change your hair color for just one day, what bold or beautiful color would you pick?

496. Who in your life holds the record for the longest marriage — and what do you admire about their bond?

497. If someone gave you a McDonald's burger-scented candle, would you light it — or toss it outside?

498. If Elvis Presley were still alive now, what stylish, wild, or surprising clothes do you think he'd be rocking?

499. What's one of the funniest or sweetest things you've ever heard a child say without realizing how funny it was?

500. Which old-school dance moves can you still pull off — and which ones make you laugh the most?

501. Have you heard a hilarious (or horrifying) story involving super glue gone wrong?

502. Do you think the full moon really affects how people act — and have you ever noticed it yourself?

503. In your view, what's the biggest risk facing humanity today — and what could we do about it?

504. Have you ever met someone who applied to drive the famous Oscar Mayer Wienermobile — or would you apply yourself?

505. If you could pick any place in the world to sleep under the stars, where would you choose?

506. Have you ever found yourself caught in the chaos of a real-life food fight — and what happened?

507. What's the weirdest or most unbelievable thing you've seen that made you do a double take?

508. If you were a top-secret spy, what fun or fierce code name would you choose for yourself?

509. Besides the sun, what's the hottest or most intense thing you've ever witnessed in nature?

510. What's your favorite fun fact you like to share when you want to spark a conversation?

511. If you had to invent a brand-new word for the Monday morning blues, what would it be?

512. If you could design your dream front door, what color and style would you choose?

513. If you could teach everyone in the world one song to sing together, which one would it be?

514. Can you remember a time you did something just to try to impress someone — and how did it go?

515. What's the most unfortunate or ridiculous tattoo you've ever spotted on another person?

516. Where were you — and what were you doing — the last time you felt completely peaceful and at ease?

517. What's the ultimate "lazy moment" you've had that still makes you laugh (or shake your head)?

518. If paparazzi mistook you for a celebrity, who would it be — and how would you handle all the sudden attention?

519. If a "DO NOT PUSH" red button was a different color, what shade would make you hesitate before pressing it?

520. How would you creatively rename a boring everyday job to make it sound grand or heroic?

521. What's the most recent thing — a sight, sound, story, or moment — that instantly caught your full attention?

522. When you're alone, do you generally feel content and at peace — or restless and eager for company?

523. In your opinion, what's the most physically or emotionally dangerous job someone could have?

524. If you had to insure one part of your body for being valuable, which part would you pick and why?

525. What's the strangest, most oddly shaped building you've ever seen or stepped inside?

526. If you could witness the launch of any great invention in history, which moment would you choose to see firsthand?

527. What are three things — big or small — that you genuinely feel proud of being good at?

528. If you were truly stuck and thirsty at home, would you swallow your pride (and a little dog water) to survive?

529. What's the most hilarious or surprising conversation you've ever accidentally overheard?

530. When was the last time you took the time to polish your shoes — and did it feel satisfying or tedious?

531. What's your favorite phrase to describe trying really hard — like "until you're blue in the face"?

532. If you had to rate your handwriting from 1 to 10, what score would you give yourself — and why?

533. In your opinion, what three things make a workout feel truly ideal — fun, challenging, rewarding?

534. How many of your family members can do the tongue curl trick — and are you among them?

535. What's the goofiest or most ridiculous country song title you've come across that still makes you laugh?

536. Would you feel excited, nervous, or skeptical about taking a trip in a completely driverless car?

537. If you had a medieval suit of armor to decorate your house, where would you proudly (or hilariously) put it?

538. What's the most delightful, silly, or surprising thing you've pulled out of a Christmas cracker?

539. Have you ever nodded off somewhere you absolutely shouldn't have — and what happened next?

540. Do you check the news daily — and what headline recently grabbed your attention most?

541. What's the silliest or most clever name you've ever heard someone give their cat?

542. If you could only have one type of flooring throughout your home, what would you pick — and why?

543. Have you ever gathered around a campfire to tell ghost stories — and what spooky tale do you remember?

544. What's something you said or did recently that might have been a little "oops" or not-so-politically-correct?

545. If you had to explain making a perfect cup of tea in just three steps, what would you say?

546. If you could superpower one of your senses — sight, hearing, taste, smell, or touch — which would you pick and why?

547. As silly as it sounds — have you ever (or known anyone who) trapped a fart in a jar just for fun?

548. If you grabbed a pen and paper right now, what picture would you naturally start sketching?

549. What's the silliest or most unnecessary warning sign you've ever spotted in real life?

550. Without looking it up, how many foods starting with "R" can you list right now?

551. Can you remember the last time you truly felt bored — and what were you doing (or avoiding)?

552. If you were a squirrel trying to outsmart other squirrels, where would you secretly stash your nuts?

553. What's the one dip you can never resist — whether for chips, veggies, or just sneaky spoonfuls?

554. Do you think athletes should be allowed to use high-tech tools or enhancements — or is that unfair?

555. What's your favorite product or treat that magically comes alive when you "just add water"?

556. In what way do you think you are most different from your parents — personality, dreams, habits?

557. If you could invent a wild new fitness trend, what crazy idea would you launch?

558. Have you ever found yourself mashing remote buttons harder and harder, even though you know the batteries are toast?

559. What's your funniest twist on the old "Why did the chicken cross the road?" joke?

560. When was the last time you did something kind for someone without expecting anything back — and what was it?

561. What's the most surprising or unique animal you've ever had the chance to hold or touch?

562. If you had to, do you think you could figure out a way to put socks on with your hands tied behind your back?

563. Who in your life would you call a "real character" — someone unforgettable — and why?

564. What's the most recent thing that made you slap your forehead and say, "I can't believe that just happened"?

565. Can you remember a time you were so caught off guard that you didn't know what to say?

566. What's one funny or ongoing thing that you and your friends always seem to disagree about?

567. If you could share a dinner with anyone in history or life today, who would you pick and why?

568. What's something hilarious or absurd that you would never expect a serious news anchor to say live on air?

569. Other than a movie character like Uncle Buck, have you ever met someone who actually microwaved their socks — or would you?

570. If you had to fill a mattress with something ridiculous, what crazy item would you choose?

571. How many people do you trust enough to share a password with — and who are they?

572. If ethics weren't a limit, what wild human experiment would you secretly find fascinating to try?

573. If you somehow discovered the true secret to staying young forever, what would it be?

574. What's an old-fashioned phrase you still find yourself saying, even though it's totally outdated?

575. What's the strangest or most unexpected type of yoga you've heard of — and would you try it?

576. If your index fingers instantly grew super long, how would that change your daily life?

577. What's the funniest or most unforgettable home video you've ever watched — or been part of?

578. Faced with an impossible choice, would you prioritize saving one child over two elderly adults?

579. What's the most blatantly sexist or outdated comment someone has said to you — and how did you respond?

580. On a scale from 1 to 10, how much do you genuinely enjoy pumpkin pie — be honest!

581. Can you remember a time when you felt butterflies or nerves walking into a building — and what was happening?

582. If you could choose any famous band to perform at your funeral celebration, who would you pick and why?

583. If you paused for a moment, what three things in your life make you feel truly grateful today?

584. Have you ever had fun pretending to be a voicemail recording — tricking someone for a laugh?

585. When you dive into a candy mix or penny sweets, which treats do you go for first without even thinking?

586. If your personality were a book genre, what would it be — mystery, adventure, fantasy, drama?

587. If clouds could appear in fun new colors instead of just white, what shades would you love to see?

588. Be honest — were you a bed bouncer when you were a kid, and how much fun did you have?

589. What's the most jaw-dropping, unbelievable thing someone ever said to you that you still can't forget?

590. Which family member has a knack for embarrassing you (lovingly or hilariously) at get-togethers?

591. If all foods tasted identical, would you still eat a variety just for texture, color, or experience?

592. Deep down, do you ever wonder or have a "hunch" about how your life story might end?

593. Have you ever gotten completely lost in a maze — and how did you find your way back?

594. What's something amazing or surprising you discovered somewhere totally boring?

595. Are you someone who sneaks a peek at the ending of a book — or do you tough it out to the last page?

596. What part of your normal day feels the most boring, repetitive, or just plain tedious?

597. If the chance came up, would you bravely take the leap and go skydiving?

598. When was the last time you had an IOU hanging over your head — and how did you pay it back?

599. If you're stuck next to someone with awful body odor on a train, how do you handle the situation?

600. If you found just one glove, what clever or silly new use could you invent for it?

601. How would having x-ray vision improve your everyday life — or just make it more interesting?

602. What everyday sound instantly brings you a sense of peace, happiness, or satisfaction?

603. How many pieces were in the largest puzzle you've ever finished — and how long did it take?

604. What's the silliest or most bizarre way you've ever heard of someone meeting their end?

605. Do you think hiding likes on social media posts would help people feel less anxious about approval?

606. Have you ever been in a situation where you felt like the biggest or most experienced person around?

607. What's the most disappointing or head-scratching gift you've ever unwrapped?

608. If you celebrate Thanksgiving, what's the heart of the holiday for you — food, family, gratitude, or fun?

609. What's something that movies love to show happening all the time — but almost never happens in real life?

610. If grass could be any color other than green, what shade would you want to see across fields and lawns?

611. If you had to keep just one kitchen appliance and give up the rest, what would you save?

612. What's the most hilarious or innocent "how babies are made" story you've ever heard?

613. Quick challenge: how many pink things can you name in ten seconds without thinking too hard?

614. What's the farthest you've ever jogged — and was it planned, spontaneous, or part of a challenge?

615. If you were a storm chaser, would you want to follow lightning, tornadoes, hurricanes, or something else?

616. What's the most recent thing that left your fingers sticky — food, glue, art project?

617. Have you ever gone on a blind date — and what's one memory that sticks out from it?

618. When you see someone experiencing homelessness, what is the first feeling or thought that crosses your mind?

619. If you could have a second home anywhere in the world, where would your dream location be?

620. Besides wiping your face, what clever or unexpected uses have you found for a handkerchief?

621. Can you remember the last time you let yourself be a kid again and jumped in a puddle?

622. If you invented a new cat food brand, what fun or clever name would you give it?

623. If you're honest with yourself, what's the biggest thing weighing on your mind today?

624. Are you a fan of marmalade sandwiches, or do you leave that love exclusively to Paddington Bear?

625. What's the wildest, weirdest, or most ridiculous gadget you've ever seen sold on TV?

626. Have you ever pretended to be clueless about something — and why did you choose to act that way?

627. What's something you tend to buy in bulk, even if it's not the fanciest version?

628. If gravity vanished for a minute, what things would you float up and bump into where you're sitting?

629. What are three experiences, moments, or goals you're most excited about in the coming year?

630. If your initials became the name of a new virus, what would it be called — and what funny or strange symptoms would it cause?

631. What's the coolest, funniest, or most surprising thing you've ever discovered hiding in the couch cushions?

632. If you could jump into a pool filled with anything fun or delicious besides water, what would you pick?

633. When's the last time you spun around, laughed too hard, or did something that made your head spin?

634. What's a completely random, probably useless fact you know that still sticks in your brain?

635. If you could design your dream house, how many rooms would it have — and what would each one be for?

636. If you were forced to eat a crayon, which color would you choose based on how "tasty" it looks?

637. Are there any songs or bands you love today that your parents also jammed out to when they were young?

638. What's the most pointless, silly, or crazy rule you've ever had to obey — even if it made no sense?

639. If Greyhound buses weren't symbolized by a greyhound, what other animal would make a cool or funny logo?

640. Who in your life do you love — but would never trust with a big secret?

641. What's the funniest or most ridiculous story you've heard about a criminal getting caught?

642. If you could decorate your house with a life-sized animal statue, which animal would you pick?

643. Which of your friends would you bet on to invent something brilliant — and what might it be?

644. On the hottest day you can remember, where were you — and how did you survive the heat?

645. If you lived a secret life as a superhero, what normal day job would you pick to hide your powers?

646. When eating a classic trifle, which layer — sponge, custard, cream, fruit — is your favorite part?

647. Do you think bands should give up world tours to help protect the planet — or is there a better solution?

648. If there were a phobia of hot dogs, what hilarious or clever name would you invent for it?

649. Have you ever ridden a Ferris wheel — and what amazing (or scary!) view did you have from the top?

650. In your view, what crime stands out as the absolute worst — and why?

651. If humans were zoo animals, what kind of habitat would we need to be happy and healthy?

652. What outdoor adventure — daring, thrilling, or peaceful — would you love to try at least once?

653. Have you ever been playfully accused of being a Grinch — and what made people think that?

654. If you could be the leader of anything — a team, a movement, a dream project — what would you choose?

655. If you could have any dessert for breakfast guilt-free, what sweet treat would you pick?

656. Thinking back, what's the last gift you ever asked Santa Claus to deliver to you?

657. What's something that sounds easy when people talk about it — but you find really hard to do?

658. What's the worst or silliest lie you've ever told — and did you get caught?

659. If your tea kettle had a voice, what funny things would it shout or whisper as it heated up?

660. If you found $20 hidden in a hotel room drawer, would you keep it, turn it in, or do something else?

661. Have you ever named your car — and what other personal items have you given names to?

662. What's the most thrilling, hilarious, or memorable adventure you've had on a waterslide?

663. If faced with the choice, would you let an animal die to save a human life — and how would you feel about it?

664. If you had to rewrite Neil Armstrong's famous moon landing line into something funny, what would you say?

665. What's the absolute worst or most awkward thing you could accidentally say on a first date?

666. Have you ever attempted the ridiculous challenge of burping the alphabet — and how far did you manage?

667. In your opinion, what ingredients — lyrics, melody, beat — make a truly unforgettable pop song?

668. How much do you find yourself caring about other people's opinions — and when does it matter most to you?

669. What's the silliest or pettiest reason you've heard for why a couple called it quits?

670. If you had to leap an eight-foot rooftop gap to survive, would you risk it — or freeze?

671. Which accent do you find irresistibly charming or attractive when you hear it spoken?

672. If you could invent a new combo utensil like the spork, what would it be and what fun name would you give it?

673. When was the last time you made a cup of tea for someone else — and what was the occasion?

674. If you invented a brand-new vegetable, what would it look like, taste like, and what name would you give it?

675. What do you think would be the toughest challenge about living alone in a tall, lonely lighthouse?

676. If you needed to fake your death and disappear, what clever or outrageous plan would you come up with?

677. What's the silliest reason you've heard of someone rushing to the ER — and did it make you laugh?

678. Whose handwriting among your friends or family members do you admire most for being super neat?

679. Have you ever peeked into the fridge to see if the light really turns off when the door closes?

680. If you opened a brand-new gym, what catchy or motivating name would you give it?

681. Do you have a favorite old pair of socks you just can't seem to throw away — and why?

682. What everyday word turns totally strange and silly when you say it over and over?

683. Have you ever attempted the impossible and tried to lick your own elbow — and did you succeed?

684. What's the wackiest or most surprising celebrity baby name you've ever heard?

685. If you could spend a day learning to cook from a top chef, which country's food would you pick to master?

686. If you could give Winnie-the-Pooh a modern makeover, what outfit would you dress him in?

687. The last time you were sick, what was it — and how did you take care of yourself?

688. If your friends had to rate your reliability from 1 to 10, what score would they give you — and why?

689. Is there a tricky crossword clue you cracked that still makes you proud when you think about it?

690. If rain ruined your picnic plans, what fun backup adventure would you create instead?

691. Look around you — what three everyday items could you turn into a musical instrument right now?

692. If you became a legendary supervillain, what awesome or funny villain name would you pick?

693. Deep down, do you believe there are more good-hearted people than bad in the world?

694. What's your funniest or wildest vacation story where everything went wrong — and you still laugh about it?

695. Have you ever dared to run up a down escalator — and how did that bold attempt end?

696. What's the wildest or most unforgettable vehicle you've ever spotted while driving or traveling?

697. When was the last time you played leapfrog — and do you think you could still pull it off today?

698. If you could only stockpile one item to prepare for staying home for a long time, what would you choose?

699. What habits or little actions do you catch yourself doing without even realizing it?

700. Who among your friends or family is the most intimidating when they lose their temper?

701. Have you ever spent a whole day lounging in bed — not because you were sick, but just because you could?

702. What's something you believed or practiced that you later had to consciously unlearn?

703. If your life were a line on paper, would it be straight, bumpy, wavy, or full of loops?

704. Which Starburst flavor makes you happiest whenever you unwrap it — and why?

705. When you make promises or set goals, how well do your actions match your words?

706. What's the wildest, most over-the-top fashion look you've ever seen on a runway?

707. When was the last time you picked up a jump rope — and do you still remember any of the old rhymes?

708. If you had to redesign the symbol of surrender, what would you wave instead of a plain white flag?

709. What appliance in your home makes the loudest, most disruptive noise — and how do you deal with it?

710. If you could sit down for a relaxed afternoon tea with any world leader, past or present, who would you choose?

711. Is there a song or piece of music you've heard way too much and would be happy never to hear again?

712. Did you ever play the silly "cooties" game in school — and who was "infected" according to your playground rules?

713. What's the last food you ate that left you running for water — salty, spicy, or something else?

714. Do you believe there's even greater happiness waiting for you in the future — and what might bring it about?

715. How many email addresses have you collected over time — and which one do you actually enjoy using?

716. If you could create a funny or fair punishment for people who leave carts everywhere, what would it be?

717. Have you ever attempted the impossible task of sneezing with your eyes open — and what happened?

718. Is there an old tech gadget you love too much to replace — even though it's way out of date?

719. When you were a kid, what was your favorite pair of pajamas — and why were they so special?

720. If you had to replace your nose with a fruit for a day, what silly or stylish fruit would you pick?

721. Can you remember a time you were so desperate for a bathroom that it felt like a real emergency?

722. What's the deepest or most hidden place underground you've ever explored — a cave, a mine, a subway tunnel?

723. If you launched a new internet search engine today, what clever or fun name would you give it?

724. What's the one pair of shoes you've owned that you loved the most — and why?

725. At what point does the cold become unbearable for you — and how do you usually cope?

726. If you could instantly master a new language, which would you choose — and how would you use it?

727. In a fun, alternate universe, what other creature (or silly thing) could replace "piggy" or "monkey" in the middle?

728. What's your most unforgettable or hilarious story involving travel sickness?

729. Are you more tuned into spotting mistakes in others' writing than catching your own?

730. Which culture do you admire from afar but think would challenge you most to live within day-to-day?

731. Who in your life truly embodies being "salt of the earth" — humble, kind, and genuine?

732. Have you ever taken scissors to a friend's hair — or would you dare if they trusted you enough?

733. If you had to swap your ears for an animal's ears, which animal would you pick — and why?

734. What's a clever mnemonic or memory trick that has stuck with you — and helped you when you needed it?

735. What affectionate names do you use (or did you use) for your grandparents?

736. When you imagine the perfect frozen yogurt, what topping absolutely has to be on it?

737. If your personality could be described as a three-course meal, what appetizer, main, and dessert would you be?

738. What three things in your home could disappear without you even realizing they were gone?

739. Have you ever made a mistake that surprisingly led to something positive or even wonderful?

740. Do you believe that banning fossil fuels is the right step toward protecting the environment — and why or why not?

741. If you could master one amazing magic trick, what would it be — and how would you use it?

742. Would you describe yourself as super competitive — or does someone else in your life outshine you there?

743. What's the strangest, most unexpected place you've ever found a lost remote control?

744. What's the wildest, funniest, or most unforgettable thing you've done because someone double-dared you?

745. Do you believe it's possible for humanity to create a future where no one goes hungry?

746. What's the most impressive or hilarious thing you've witnessed someone balancing on their head?

747. Look around you: would the object closest to you help you survive a zombie attack?

748. If you could turn any food into a spreadable form, what would you love to smear on toast?

749. When did you last dive into a crunchy, colorful pile of leaves — and how did it feel?

750. If you could design a silly crop circle, what hilarious pattern would you leave for the world to wonder about?

751. Has there ever been a game — board, card, video, or sport — you found impossible to stop playing?

752. What movie from the past year do you think deserves a Golden Raspberry Award for being wonderfully bad?

753. Do you still have a collection of CDs — and can you remember the last one you bought?

754. What's the most shocking or heartbreaking story of medical malpractice you've ever heard about?

755. If you could pick any style of designer sunglasses to wear, what would they look like?

756. If we had to stop saying "raining cats and dogs," what funny or magical thing should it rain instead?

757. Have you ever smiled and nodded along when you had no idea what someone was talking about? What was it?

758. What special accessories turn a good snowman into a perfect snowman?

759. If you had to face three crocodiles to win a million dollars, would you risk it — or find another way?

760. What's the weirdest or funniest thing you've ever pulled out of a jacket or pants pocket by surprise?

761. If you had to nominate someone you know to win a belly dancing contest, who would it be?

762. Do you think Bigfoot might really exist — or is it just a fun story to you?

763. What's something you recently gave yourself a hard time about — even though you know you should be kind to yourself?

764. If you had to migrate like a bird for the winter, where would you choose to spend the cold months?

765. Aside from your birthday, what day of the year feels extra special to you — and why?

766. If you could choose, what memorable or meaningful final words would you want to leave behind?

767. If you could invent a brand-new, silly name for an incredibly huge number, what would you call it?

768. What's a powerful or meaningful piece of advice or wisdom someone once shared with you?

769. If you invented a new non-alcoholic drink, what fun ingredients would you include — and what would you name it?

770. In a moment of frustration, what's the wildest or funniest thing you've ever hurled across a room?

771. Do you think the world will ever discover the true identity behind the mysterious artist Banksy?

772. Can you think of a product that solves a problem nobody really had — but somehow became popular anyway?

773. If telling a lie made your pants literally catch fire today, how badly would you be burned?

774. Have you ever had a moment of pure excitement or chaos where you just wanted to let loose completely?

775. When was the last time you hopped on a bike — and how did it make you feel?

776. If you could rename a Hershey's Kiss, what new and fun name would you choose?

777. Which part of astronaut training — from zero-gravity drills to simulations — do you think you'd ace?

778. If you had to deliver a 20-minute presentation with no prep, what topic would you feel confident speaking about?

779. Which YouTuber do you find yourself watching the most often — and why do you like their content?

780. How would you rate your personal "weirdness" on a scale of 1 to 10 — and are you proud of it?

781. What's your favorite word that sounds like the thing it describes — like "buzz" or "pop"?

782. If you had to pick a cowboy name for yourself, what would it be — tough, funny, or legendary?

783. When was the last time you hopped into a lively conga line — and where was the party?

784. If you could have anything magically delivered to your door right now, what would you wish for?

785. Imagine you found a brand-new plant species — what would it look like, and what creative name would you give it?

786. What experience, moment, or simple pleasure feels like pure bliss to you?

787. Which friend or family member do you think has the best balance or focus to win a plate-spinning contest?

788. What three things do you think adults have that kids are always eager (or impatient) to get?

789. If Big Ben could chime something fun instead of its traditional "bong," what sound would you choose?

790. If you could transform into any vehicle, what awesome machine would you become — car, plane, something wild?

791. What's a healthy outlet you use (or could use) to let out frustration and feel better afterward?

792. How expressive are you with just your face and body — how many emotions could you act out without words?

793. What's a current trend or craze that totally puzzles you — you just don't see the appeal?

794. How long do you think you could realistically hold a plank — and would you ever want to beat your record?

795. If you could spend one day in any historical era, which period would you visit and why?

796. If you had to fire a friend from a job, how would you handle it with honesty and care?

797. When a cramp strikes, what's your go-to tip or trick to ease the pain quickly?

798. Have you ever had a classic stumble over untied laces — and what happened afterward?

799. What's the funniest, most creative, or most memorable voicemail message you've ever heard?

800. Are there any small habits or rituals you find yourself doing automatically, even when you don't think about them?

801. Do you think the internet could ever truly "break" — and if so, what might be the cause?

802. If you could only have one piece of exercise equipment at home, what would you pick to stay healthy and happy?

803. Have you ever admired someone so much you put them on a pedestal — and do you still see them that way?

804. If you had to compare the shape of your country to something fun or creative, what would it be?

805. Have you ever tried a diet that was so awful you couldn't wait to quit — and what made it so bad?

806. If you had braces, how did you celebrate when they finally came off — and what was the first thing you ate?

807. What topping would turn a plain bowl of Shredded Wheat into a perfect, crave-worthy breakfast?

808. If your pets had to describe your qualities for a job, would they recommend you — and what would they say?

809. What was the most recent secret Santa gift you picked — and how did you choose it?

810. Have you ever attempted to twerk — even just for fun — and how did it go?

811. If you could explore the center of the Earth, what's the wildest or weirdest thing you imagine finding there?

812. Do you believe the world could eliminate single-use plastics during your lifetime — and what would help it happen?

813. What's the most ridiculous or risky object you've ever stood on to reach something way up high?

814. What other delicious foods are so rich, spicy, or indulgent they deserve a "danger of death" label?

815. Where were you when your stomach made loud, awkward noises at exactly the wrong time?

816. Do you think the phrase "having a blonde moment" is offensive, and why or why not?

817. What's the most hilarious or strange real place name you've come across?

818. When was the last time you paused and noticed the sound of birds — and what did it make you feel?

819. If you invented a carpet shampoo with the perfect smell, what would it smell like and what would you call it?

820. What's the most clever or high-scoring word you've proudly crafted during a Scrabble game?

821. Who in your life is the true champion of making the most of an all-you-can-eat buffet?

822. What's the most toe-curling, eye-watering object you've ever stepped on barefoot?

823. Do you believe "common sense" is still common — or is it rarer than we like to think?

824. Which world event today would be the hardest for you to explain simply to a young child?

825. If James Bond swapped his famous martini for something silly, what drink would make you laugh most?

826. If you had to run a three-legged race with a friend, who would you trust most to stay in sync with you?

827. Have you ever accidentally spoken your thoughts aloud — and what happened next?

828. What's the funniest or most creative expression you've ever heard for "going to the bathroom"?

829. How would you handle sitting next to a crying baby on a long flight when patience is running low?

830. Do you believe in karma — that good and bad actions eventually come back around?

831. What's the most memorable or hilarious experience you've had during a team-building activity?

832. If you were magically turned into a tree, would you want to be tall and towering or small and cozy?

833. If you discovered a brand-new galaxy, what imaginative or playful name would you give it?

834. If you could have one major home upgrade done by professionals, what would you choose?

835. Have you ever taken or would you like to take a pilgrimage — and where would your heart lead you?

836. Do you think science will one day figure out how to make humans live forever — and should we?

837. Can you beatbox — or what's the best funny sound you can make if you try?

838. When you think of Scotland, what are the first three things, images, or ideas that pop into your mind?

839. Do you think famous athletes should leave social media to protect their mental health from racism?

840. If you had to choose a bright new skin color, what vibrant shade would you rock with pride?

841. What's the most incredible or heart-stopping escape story you've ever come across?

842. When was the last time you visited a library — and what did you discover or borrow?

843. Do you believe stealing can ever be justified — and if so, under what circumstances?

844. If a real Jurassic Park opened today, would you be brave (or curious) enough to visit?

845. What's the most clever or spiteful (but not harmful) revenge story you've heard?

846. Have you ever had the eerie feeling that someone was watching you — and what were the circumstances?

847. If you could build your own "Magnificent Seven" dream team, who would you choose to ride alongside you?

848. Do you happen to share a birthday with any well-known celebrities or historical figures?

849. What's the wildest or funniest story you've ever heard related to a bizarre car insurance claim?

850. Do you think online shopping will eventually replace traditional stores — or will in-person shopping survive?

851. Which actor's attempt at a music career do you think was the most cringe-worthy or surprising?

852. Do you think expelling students from school is a fair solution — and under what circumstances, if any?

853. How do you prefer to keep track of important dates and appointments — a planner, phone calendar, or something else?

854. Can you remember a moment when you had to set aside your pride and do something difficult?

855. What's one of the scariest things you've ever lived through — or witnessed happen to someone else?

856. Have you ever hidden something important "somewhere safe" — only to completely forget where it was?

857. If you could choose, what would be the most adventurous, creative, or heroic way to go out?

858. If laughter is the ultimate cure, what would you name as the next best thing for the soul?

859. When it comes to milkshakes, what's the one flavor you always crave?

860. Would you ever volunteer for a paid clinical trial — and how much money would make it worth it for you?

861. What's the funniest or most embarrassing autocorrect mistake you've ever accidentally sent?

862. If you had to lose a body part — but not an essential one — what would you miss the least?

863. Have you ever carried a lucky charm or special object for good luck? What was it?

864. What's the last item you purchased simply because it made you smile, even though you didn't "need" it?

865. Have you ever had the unlucky (or hilarious) experience of getting pooped on by a bird or animal?

866. What are your three go-to websites when you're browsing or buying things online?

867. If you had to pick someone NOT to watch your house or pets, who would it be — and what's your reason?

868. What's a time when words really hurt you — and how did you move past it?

869. If you created a new candy bar by mixing three favorites together, what would you name it?

870. What's something you just can't bring yourself to believe, no matter how many times you hear it?

871. Were there any school-assigned books that you genuinely enjoyed reading?

872. Who's a person you think would be the absolute worst candidate for US President today?

873. Have you ever felt deeply misunderstood by someone — and what was the situation?

874. What's the funniest or most shocking story you know about someone swallowing something they definitely shouldn't have?

875. If you had to redesign Little Red Riding Hood's cloak, what new color would you pick — and why?

876. What's the most elegant or beautiful garden ornament you've ever come across?

877. Do you keep recipe books at home — and is there one that you reach for more than the others?

878. If you could create your own cologne, what would it smell like — and what catchy or elegant name would you give it?

879. What's the most unplanned, spur-of-the-moment thing you've ever done — and how did it turn out?

880. If you could invent a fun or silly name for the skin on your nose, what would you call it?

881. In your view, what special qualities make us truly human — beyond biology?

882. If you could have one question about your life's future answered right now, what would you want to know?

883. When was the last time you got completely muddy — and how did it happen?

884. What's the strangest or funniest "Top 5" list you've ever seen or heard about?

885. If you could only eat raw foods, what cooked meals would you miss the most?

886. If you could celebrate New Year's Eve anywhere in the world with friends, where would you go?

887. What's the smartest or funniest name you've ever seen on a restaurant sign?

888. Do you believe humans are the most advanced beings out there — or do you think we have cosmic company?

889. Have you ever faced a moment where doing the "right thing" still felt wrong somehow?

890. Thinking back, what was the most intense pain you've ever felt — and how would you rate it out of ten?

891. What's a product or invention you think is completely useless — even if it's funny?

892. When was a time you surprised yourself (or others) by pulling off a last-minute solution?

893. If you had to replace your last name with a food, what delicious or funny name would you choose?

894. What three actions or betrayals do you personally find almost impossible to forgive?

895. Have you ever helped someone by trimming their toenails — and would you do it again if needed?

896. What's the most snobbish or out-of-touch thing you've ever overheard someone say?

897. If you had to pick a fun or bold color for a dental implant instead of white, what would you go for?

898. What's something you seem to buy way less often than the people around you?

899. Do you think anything that happened to you this week will still stand out a year from now?

900. Have you ever had a stay-at-home vacation (staycation) that turned into an amazing memory?

901. Has anyone ever been way off when guessing your age — either thinking you were younger or older?

902. What's the biggest tip you've ever given to thank someone for outstanding service?

903. If you had to turn one of your online usernames into a band name, which one would sound coolest?

904. What's the coolest or funniest science experiment you've ever tried outside of school?

905. Do you believe some people deserve a third chance — and under what circumstances would you give it?

906. Have you ever had a super awkward silence where you could practically hear the "tumbleweeds"? What happened?

907. If your personality could be a vacation spot, where would it be — sunny, adventurous, cozy, or exciting?

908. Whose celebrity home made you wonder what they were thinking when it came to decorating?

909. If you could get VIP tickets to any event in the world, which one would you be thrilled to attend?

910. What's the highest building you've ever stood atop — and what did you see or feel up there?

911. Who in your life do you admire for really embracing every moment and living life to the fullest?

912. If potatoes were your star ingredient, what creative or delicious dish would you cook up?

913. Do you believe in the existence of ghosts — and have you ever experienced something you couldn't explain?

914. What's the silliest or most surprising design you've ever spotted on a shower curtain?

915. Should cultural institutions accept sponsorship from fossil-fuel companies — or should they refuse?

916. Have you ever experienced first class on a flight — and if not, which airline would you dream of trying?

917. What's the strangest or most bizarre item you've ever seen advertised for sale — online or in a shop?

918. If you could invent any app to make life more fun, easy, or meaningful, what would it do?

919. What's the most chilling or unsettling true crime story you've ever come across?

920. What's the most you've let the dishes pile up before finally tackling the mountain of plates?

921. In your view, what's the rudest behavior someone can show in everyday life?

922. Were you ever bullied in school — and does the memory of the bully still stick with you?

923. What's the most uncomfortable thing you've done just to be polite — and was it worth it?

924. Do you think it's possible to truly understand happiness if you've never felt sadness?

925. If you had to invent a rapper name for yourself, what cool or funny name would you pick?

926. In what area of your life do you sometimes struggle most with staying disciplined?

927. What's a shocking scientific experiment from history that could never be done today?

928. Have you ever experienced seasickness — and where were you when it happened?

929. What's the most random, silly, or unexpected thing you've thrown into your cart at the store?

930. Do you usually meet the recommended exercise goal each week — or fall a little short?

931. What's the most amazing or jaw-dropping magic trick you've ever seen?

932. If you worked as a wildlife videographer, what magical moment would you dream of capturing?

933. What's the creepiest or most mysterious sound you've ever heard — and where were you?

934. Have you ever taken a dip in a river — and what was the experience like?

935. What's the most awkward or inappropriate question someone has asked you — and how did you respond?

936. Can you remember the last time something made you look twice because you couldn't believe your eyes?

937. What's one truly amazing or mind-blowing fact you know about how the human body works?

938. Did you grow up wearing hand-me-downs — and how do you feel about secondhand clothes today?

939. What's the weirdest or most creative name you've ever seen on a paint color label?

940. Who comes to mind when you think of someone truly sophisticated — in style, speech, or manners?

941. What's the weirdest or funniest compliment you've ever received — and how did you react?

942. Have you ever realized after a long time that you'd been calling someone by the wrong name?

943. What's the longest you've gone without bathing — and what was the reason?

944. Which celebrities do you admire for their fashion sense or personal style?

945. What's the boldest or most extreme thing you've ever dared yourself to try?

946. Do the songs you loved a decade ago still hold a special place in your playlist?

947. If someone near you was bleeding heavily, would you know how to help — and have you ever needed to?

948. Do you think the horror genre still has a place in movies, or should it be left behind?

949. What little habit or quirk about your personality would you change if you could?

950. If you woke up from a long winter's nap like a bear, what meal would you crave first?

951. What's the last flat-pack furniture or kit you assembled — and how did it go?

952. What's something you believe should be free for all people but still costs money today?

953. Have you ever navigated somewhere using a paper map instead of GPS — and how did it go?

954. Is there a family member's name you're secretly relieved not to have been given?

955. What's the weirdest or grossest old healing method you've ever heard of from history?

956. If you ran out of plates during a party, what creative thing would you use to serve food?

957. Do you have a funny or memorable school science project that completely went wrong?

958. If you had to have an extra arm, leg, or something else, what would you choose and why?

959. What funny or unusual names would you give to the three bears in the Goldilocks story?

960. Do you think having too many options can sometimes make decisions harder instead of easier?

961. What three simple things help you truly feel like the weekend has started?

962. Do you feel older, younger, or exactly your real age when you think about yourself on the inside?

963. What's the most extreme or heartbreaking story you've heard about hoarding?

964. If you could rename vegetarian bacon with a creative name, what would you call it?

965. What's the last gadget, toy, or tool you had to put new batteries in?

966. Have you ever bought something from a late-night infomercial — and did it live up to the hype?

967. What's the funniest, silliest, or most surprising brand name you've ever come across?

968. Is there a classic board game you now prefer to play online or on an app instead of in person?

969. What types of things tend to move you to tears — happy, sad, inspiring, or unexpected moments?

970. If you had to rename "Toot Sweets" from Chitty Chitty Bang Bang, what fun new name would you pick?

971. What's the most surprising and expensive repair bill you've ever been hit with?

972. When was the last time you covered your eyes during a TV show or movie — and what was happening?

973. How does your routine or home environment change when you're preparing to host guests?

974. When you play "rock, paper, scissors," do you say "shoot" at the end, or skip it?

975. Can you remember the most completely lost you've ever been — and where it happened?

976. If you could throw a party somewhere totally unexpected, where would your dream location be?

977. What's your favorite (or funniest) memory from a school field day?

978. Have you ever gone skinny dipping — and when and where did it happen?

979. What's the best or most memorable message you've ever pulled from a fortune cookie?

980. Who in your life or in the world do you see as a truly daring and courageous real-life hero?

981. Which of your friends has the funniest or most unique laugh — and what does it sound like?

982. What music has been your personal soundtrack today — and how has it matched your mood?

983. If you could combine two dog breeds to create a fun new name like "labradoodle," what would you choose?

984. What's your favorite riddle — one that's fun to share or still makes people think?

985. If you had to have a visible scar from stitches, where would you want it to be and why?

986. What's a movie you found totally over-the-top or silly — but you enjoyed it anyway?

987. If you could mash together three different sports into one crazy new game, which ones would you choose?

988. Looking back, what's something you spent time on that you now see as a total waste?

989. Have you ever quoted "Life is like a box of chocolates" — and in what situation did it feel true?

990. If you could invent a word to describe the sound of cheese melting, what would it be?

991. If you discovered a brand-new chemical element, what creative or powerful name would you give it?

992. If you had magic cream that could make anything disappear with one dab, what would you choose to erase?

993. What's one exciting or joyful thing that happened to you this year that still makes you smile?

994. If you could get free food for life from one restaurant or chain, which one would you choose?

995. Where have you traveled or explored that felt completely new, adventurous, or unknown to you?

996. What's the absolute worst or strangest thing you can imagine putting inside a sandwich?

997. Do you believe there are situations where it's right to take justice into your own hands?

998. How do you imagine the meeting of an unstoppable force and an immovable object — and what does it mean to you?

999. If snakes were soft and furry instead of scaly, would you feel differently about them?

1000. If you had to make up a funny or weird line no one would expect in a Star Wars movie, what would it be?

1001. Without looking it up, how many cities starting with the letter "B" can you list?

1002. If a cashier accidentally gives you too much change, what do you believe is the right thing to do?

1003. If you had to secretly hide 101 dalmatians in your home, where would you try to stash them?

1004. If Harry Potter needed a silly new name for his magical adventures, what would you call him?

1005. Have you ever passed along a gift you received to someone else — and what was it?

1006. When you retire someday, what hobbies or activities would you love to spend more time doing?

1007. If someone says they hate haters, does that make them a hater too — or something different?

1008. In your opinion, which movie has the most spectacular or unforgettable explosion scene?

1009. Is there someone you know who confidently believes they're much smarter than they really are?

1010. What was the most recent birthday gift you chose for someone — and why did you pick it?

1011. Have you ever faced a moment where having too many choices made it harder, not easier?

1012. If your current mood were a picture or a scene, what would it look like?

1013. When in your life did you have the longest hair you've ever had — and what made you change it?

1014. How can people tell when you're feeling stressed — what signs do you usually show?

1015. When your phone rings with an unknown number, do you pick it up or let it go to voicemail?

1016. If someone across from you at dinner is loudly smacking their lips, how do you handle it?

1017. If you had to hide a life-size cutout of The Rock somewhere at home, where would you stash him?

1018. What sounds instantly make you cringe or feel uncomfortable — nails on a chalkboard, anyone?

1019. When was the last time you got a case of hiccups — and what trick worked to stop them?

1020. When you play Monopoly, which token do you always hope to get, and why?

1021. Can you remember a time when you truly understood someone else's experience by seeing it from their view?

1022. What's something you almost committed to — but changed your mind about at the very last moment?

1023. If you had to convince people that an unhealthy food was actually good for them, how would you sell it?

1024. Which classic nursery rhyme can you still recite perfectly from memory?

1025. Are you someone who tends to hold onto grudges — and is there one you're still carrying today?

1026. What's the funniest, most awkward, or most memorable moment you've had in a public changing room?

1027. If you could hypnotize a family member just for fun, what harmless thing would you make them do?

1028. Is there a nickname or sweet term people use that secretly drives you crazy?

1029. Have you ever let yourself be persuaded into something you didn't want to do — and what happened?

1030. What are the three qualities you value most when choosing and keeping close friends?

1031. Is there any canned fruit you actually prefer over fresh, and why?

1032. What's the most iconic guitar riff that you think everyone should know?

1033. How conscious are you of using single-use items — and how could you cut down?

1034. What's your go-to dad joke that always gets a laugh — or at least a groan?

1035. Which famous chef's menu would feel like a nightmare meal for you — and why?

1036. What's a fun or useful skill you believe you could learn well in just 30 days?

1037. If Middle Earth were real, where on Earth would you imagine it hiding?

1038. If someone is clearly bluffing at a gathering, do you call them out, ignore it, or play along?

1039. If you could rename guinea pigs based on what they really are, what fun new name would you give them?

1040. When you need comfort, what's the first food you crave?

1041. When was the last time you walked barefoot outside, and how did it feel?

1042. What's the priciest meal you've ever splurged on, and was it worth it?

1043. Who's the most creatively eccentric person you know — and what makes them unique?

1044. What small thing tends to make you feel uneasy, suspicious, or overly cautious?

1045. What's the most slices of toast you've eaten at once — and could you top that number today?

1046. What type of facial hair style do you think looks the best — on yourself or others?

1047. Did you have chickenpox as a child, and what tricks did your family use to help you stop scratching?

1048. What pet did you dream of having as a child — but never got?

1049. If there were no money, what would be your favorite way to be rewarded for your work?

1050. What's something you felt absolutely certain about recently — big or small?

1051. Have you ever jokingly called someone "Fancy-Pants" — and what outfit inspired it?

1052. What's the most stomach-turning sound you've ever heard — and how did you react?

1053. Is there a friend you love but secretly wish had a mute button sometimes — just for a moment?

1054. If you could instantly master any martial art, which style would you choose and why?

1055. What's the most memorable or funny scene you've witnessed while people-watching at an airport?

1056. When you spot a spider on your wall, do you save it, squish it, or run away?

1057. What's a food you eat often but have never actually seen in its original, natural form?

1058. How many clocks are in your home — and are they all set correctly, or are some a little off?

1059. If you could bring back any souvenir from a country you visit, what would you want it to be?

1060. If your personality were a dog breed, which one would match you best?

1061. What unexpected scent would you love (or laugh at) in a bar of soap?

1062. What's the strangest item you've ever seen someone use as a hair tie?

1063. Is there a conspiracy theory you secretly think might have a little truth behind it?

1064. In your opinion, what's the best age range to become a parent and why?

1065. Do you see yourself as an artistic person — and what creative outlet do you enjoy most?

1066. If you had an empty ice cream container, what imaginative new use would you find for it?

1067. If royalty visited your home for tea, what special or fun treats would you serve?

1068. What big world problem do you think technology could realistically fix in the next five years?

1069. Do you keep a personal journal or diary — and how often do you like to write in it?

1070. What's the funniest or most unusual family name you've ever heard?

1071. When was the last time you felt nervous and excited all at once — like having butterflies in your stomach?

1072. What's something you've done recently that made you realize, "I'm becoming just like my mom or dad"?

1073. Do you believe people should be treated as innocent until proven guilty — and why?

1074. What's your favorite hand shadow puppet to make — and can you teach it to others?

1075. Who's the boldest, wildest, or most unforgettable performer you've ever seen live?

1076. What's your favorite food to throw on the barbecue or grill when it's time to cook outdoors?

1077. If you had to design an outfit using curtains, which room's curtains would you choose and why?

1078. What's the last meal or treat you made completely from scratch — and how did it turn out?

1079. If someone offered you $1,000 to try a ski jump, would you accept the challenge?

1080. What's the most impressive or fun basketball trick shot you've ever seen?

1081. Which of your friends can do the most wicked or hilarious evil laugh?

1082. What's the most clever, funny, or memorable email address you've come across?

1083. Have you ever let loose and danced or sang in the rain? What was it like?

1084. Which land animal would be amazing to watch swimming underwater if it could?

1085. If you became a WWE wrestler, what tough or funny name would you choose for yourself?

1086. If you had to play the role of a fictional assassin, who would you pretend to target (fictional, not real)?

1087. Do you think robots could ever truly replace human teachers in schools — why or why not?

1088. What three qualities matter most to you when choosing a real, true friend?

1089. If you accidentally swallowed a fly, would you laugh, panic, or just move on?

1090. Have you ever walked out of a movie before it finished — and what made you leave?

1091. If you were on the Titanic, what plan would you have used to get a spot on a lifeboat?

1092. What's a delicious food from another country you wish you could find where you live?

1093. What short saying or belief best captures how you try to live your life?

1094. Have you ever traveled somewhere so remote it felt like you were completely off the map?

1095. Do you believe the saying "all's fair in love and war" is true — why or why not?

1096. Have you ever tried flipping a pancake — and how did it go?

1097. How many songs can you name that mention a number in the title or words?

1098. When you couldn't find a pen, what unusual object did you use to write with?

1099. If you could watch a movie told from a different character's perspective, which one would you pick?

1100. What's the most impressive thing you've seen a trained animal accomplish?

1101. If you could magically make one part of your body a little bigger, what would you choose?

1102. What do you imagine would happen if a vampire bit a zombie?

1103. Have you ever flown a kite, and what do you remember about your last time doing it?

1104. What's the funniest, coolest, or most creative car sunshade you've ever spotted?

1105. Do you believe in love at first sight — and have you ever experienced it yourself?

1106. How low do you let your phone battery get before you rush to plug it in?

1107. Can you think of a moment in your life when you knew there was no turning back?

1108. If not by wealth or fame, how should we truly measure success?

1109. If you could create any gadget to save time in daily life, what would it help with?

1110. If someone is tailgating you on the road, how do you handle it safely and calmly?

1111. Would you gamble a smaller prize for a much bigger one if you were almost sure you could win?

1112. What's the most unlikely name you could imagine for a royal baby?

1113. If you're with a group and there's only one slice of pizza left, what's your move?

1114. What small, annoying thing threw off your day a little bit today?

1115. Have you ever gotten a mystery Valentine — and never found out who sent it?

1116. If you could name a racing greyhound, what fast, fun name would you choose?

1117. Which celebrity do you think the world might be better off without — and why?

1118. What big world event from your lifetime do you think future kids will study in school?

1119. Who has had the biggest impact on your life that you're most grateful for?

1120. What is one rule you believe should always be honored, no matter what?

1121. If you moved somewhere new, what would be your best way to make new friends?

1122. In a parallel world, what funny or surprising materials could the three little pigs have used for their houses?

1123. When did you last have a snowball fight — and who were you battling against?

1124. If you competed on a baking show, what special bake would you want to be known for?

1125. Do you have a piece of jewelry or a watch that has been passed down in your family?

1126. What's the strangest place or item you've ever had to sleep on?

1127. Have you ever wished on a star — and did the wish actually come true?

1128. What song feels like your personal anthem — the one that speaks to who you are?

1129. If a new month was added to the year, what creative name would you give it?

1130. What three things would you be willing to give up right now to gain the one thing you truly want most?

1131. How active are you during a typical day — do you ever aim for 10,000 steps?

1132. What team name would be funny or tricky for cheerleaders to try and chant or spell out?

1133. If you could follow anyone for a day to learn from them, who would you choose and why?

1134. What's the last time you did something competitive — and how did it go?

1135. If money wasn't a limit, where would you treat yourself to dinner tonight?

1136. What sights, sounds, or memories easily make you feel sentimental?

1137. Have you ever learned a word that means something totally different in another part of the world?

1138. What's the smartest or funniest comeback you've heard when someone teased about height?

1139. Which friend stands out as the most confident, bold, and unapologetically loud?

1140. If you were a writer, what pen name would you choose — and why?

1141. What do you think could realistically threaten the future of humanity?

1142. If you starred in a biopic, which real-life person would you love to portray?

1143. What's the funniest or most memorable story you have involving a hot tub?

1144. If you could redesign New York City's cabs, what fun or striking color would you pick?

1145. What's a word you find simply delightful, funny, or satisfying to say out loud?

1146. Have you ever accidentally forgotten a family member's birthday — and how did you make it up to them?

1147. If you had to create a fun or clever rival company to compete with Amazon, what would you call it?

1148. Do you believe being an only child means missing out — or does it create different kinds of opportunities?

1149. If you could make up a word for one of your quirks or habits, what would it be?

1150. If you could step inside any video game for one day, which world would you want to explore?

1151. What childhood games did you love that today's kids might not even know about?

1152. Have you ever wanted to be in two places at once — and what were the places?

1153. When you can't fall asleep, what are your go-to tricks or rituals to help you relax?

1154. If you could get a behind-the-scenes tour of any place in the world, where would you pick and why?

1155. Have you ever dipped a cookie or biscuit in tea (or coffee) — and do you love or hate it?

1156. What's the most recent do-it-yourself project you tackled — and how did it go?

1157. How did you choose to celebrate your most recent birthday — big, small, or special in some way?

1158. What monument or famous place have you seen illuminated at night that took your breath away?

1159. When was the last time you had a nosebleed, and what were you doing at the time?

1160. If someone stole food off your plate, what funny or fair punishment would you give them?

1161. If you couldn't drink water, what would be your next go-to drink to quench your thirst?

1162. What's something you accomplished recently that you couldn't help but share?

1163. If you could design your own Lego set, what theme or world would you create?

1164. If you had to accept a superpower you didn't really want, what would it be — and why?

1165. If the legendary city of Atlantis exists, where do you think it might be hidden?

1166. What would your personal version of paradise look, feel, and sound like?

1167. If you could invent a new slogan for a sportswear brand, what catchy phrase would you create?

1168. What five personal or cultural treasures would you lock away in a time capsule for future discovery?

1169. If your home's power depended on pedaling a bike, what changes would you make in your daily life?

1170. If you faced an angry elephant running toward you, what would be your survival plan?

1171. Have you ever found out something way later than everyone else? What was it?

1172. What's the loudest, most ear-shattering sound you've ever heard in real life?

1173. If you were called for jury duty on a major case, would you serve or try to get out of it?

1174. What's the last item you bought or donated to a secondhand or thrift store?

1175. Who among your friends is always bursting with ideas, big or small?

1176. What's your go-to snack when you get hungry in the middle of the afternoon?

1177. What items do you usually have tucked in your pockets — and how many are there?

1178. What cool feature do you predict all cars will have in the future?

1179. Is there a cause you believe in enough that you would join a protest march for it?

1180. What moment, tradition, or feeling makes you feel proud of your country?

1181. Have you ever laughed after hitting your funny bone — even though it hurt?

1182. What's your favorite food that you can eat on a stick?

1183. If you were stranded without a phone, would you try to hitchhike for help?

1184. What's the longest you've ever had to wait on hold — and how did you pass the time?

1185. How many appliances or gadgets do you leave plugged in all the time?

1186. If you spot someone with toilet paper stuck to their shoe, do you tell them or stay silent?

1187. Should the ancient sport of jousting be revived and added to the Olympics?

1188. What's the funniest or most unexpected disaster you've had trying a home remedy?

1189. What food or drink is your hometown especially known for?

1190. What's something you think humanity has lost that may never be recovered?

1191. Who would you love to have by your side celebrating your 90th birthday?

1192. If you could get a signed photo from anyone, living or historic, who would it be?

1193. If you could name a hurricane, what new name would you suggest?

1194. If Smurfs needed a new name today, what fun or creative name would you invent?

1195. What's a funny or embarrassing song lyric you misunderstood the first time you heard it?

1196. When you were little, what treats did you leave out for Santa and his reindeer?

1197. What's the funniest prank you've heard about involving identical twins?

1198. If you competed as an Olympic swimmer, which stroke would you dominate in?

1199. If you could change three things about your current job, what would they be?

1200. When did you last give someone flowers, and what was the occasion?

1201. If Yankee Doodle lived in a parallel universe, what silly thing would he stick in his cap instead of a feather?

1202. Have you ever woken up and spent part of your day thinking a dream was real?

1203. If you could invent a new phrase for a candy heart, what sweet or funny saying would you choose?

1204. If you found yourself buried under an avalanche, what survival steps would you take?

1205. If you had to choose one of the seven dwarfs to represent you, who would it be and why?

1206. What's the funniest or most clever custom license plate you've ever spotted?

1207. Have you met someone who overuses confusing tech jargon in everyday conversation?

1208. What special experience would you love to feel again for the very first time?

1209. Have you ever been told something you wish you didn't know? What was it?

1210. How do you handle it when you need to introduce someone but forget their name?

1211. What's the strangest real-life job you've ever heard about?

1212. What's the last important thing you accidentally deleted? How did you react?

1213. If you had to swap your right foot for an animal's, which animal's foot would you pick?

1214. What rare or magical experience would you love to live through again?

1215. In your opinion, who deserves the title of "King of Pop" today?

1216. If you could invent a brand-new emoji, what would it look like and when would you use it?

1217. If you could have one absolute guarantee in life, what would you choose to be sure of?

1218. In a parallel universe, what could Hogwarts teach instead of magic?

1219. Do you believe that fate plays a role in how life unfolds? Why or why not?

1220. How do you politely get away when someone just won't stop talking?

1221. If you could have a body part make a funny warning sound like a rattlesnake, which part would you choose?

1222. What's the worst haircut you've ever had — and how did you handle it?

1223. What two unlikely talents would make an amazing and funny performance when combined?

1224. Which movie have you seen the most times, and how many watches are you at?

1225. Have you ever gotten teary-eyed because of a commercial? What was it about?

1226. What's the last activity you did that really made you break a sweat?

1227. How would your life feel different if there were no music at all?

1228. If you could put a message inside a chocolate wrapper to brighten someone's day, what would it say?

1229. If you had to turn an everyday item into a secret spy gadget, what would you choose?

1230. What hand signal do you think everyone across the world recognizes?

1231. Would you ever dare to pet or touch a cockroach if someone dared you?

1232. What's the last meeting, event, or plan you had to cancel — and why?

1233. Is there a chair, couch spot, or seat in your home that's unofficially "claimed" by someone?

1234. What's something that popped back into your mind recently that you wish had stayed forgotten?

1235. If you had to be stuck in an elevator with a celebrity, who would you want it to be?

1236. What's the longest bridge you've ever crossed, and where was it located?

1237. Do you think people making very high salaries should be required to donate to charity? Why or why not?

1238. What's the longest time you've spent not speaking to someone you care about — and why?

1239. If you had to run away from danger right now, how far do you think you'd make it?

1240. If you could be a Guinness World Record holder, what amazing or funny record would you want?

1241. Do you believe happiness is something you choose, or something that just happens?

1242. When did you last give or receive a handmade gift — and what made it special?

1243. If The Lion, the Witch and the Wardrobe had a parallel universe title, what would it be?

1244. How many things do you still unlock with a physical key — and which one would be the hardest to replace?

1245. What's the strangest or funniest thing you've ever seen tied to the roof of a moving car?

1246. In your opinion, how many kids is the tipping point from "big family" to "too many"?

1247. If you could invent a new jelly bean flavor, what would it be?

1248. If a song played every time you sneezed, what song would you pick?

1249. What's something that never fails to make you smile when you see it?

1250. Do you think live music feels better when it's played outside? Why or why not?

1251. What's your favorite trick for getting yourself awake and moving in the morning?

1252. Have you ever gone to the movies by yourself? If not, would you try it?

1253. If you could have any piece of jewelry — cost no issue — what would you pick?

1254. If you could pick anyone for a fun water pistol duel, who would you choose?

1255. What's the single file on your computer that you absolutely can't afford to lose?

1256. Has curiosity ever led you into unexpected or funny trouble? What happened?

1257. Which Google Doodle has been your favorite and why did it stand out to you?

1258. If you were ever mistakenly arrested, what do you think it would be for?

1259. If you could write a message for a greeting card, what kind of verse would you create?

1260. What old-school slang word would you love to see become popular again?

1261. If you could grant one wish for someone else, what would you wish for them?

1262. What are three types of things you always check reviews for before buying?

1263. What brand or model was your very first cell phone?

1264. If given the opportunity to live at the ISS for six months, would you accept?

1265. Can you recall the last time you stood up for someone else? What happened?

1266. If Nike had to change its brand name, what creative new name would you suggest?

1267. What's the funniest or most memorable thing that's happened to you at a gym or fitness class?

1268. Have you ever accidentally discovered a secret you weren't meant to know? What was it?

1269. Which device do you mostly use to capture photos — your phone, camera, or something else?

1270. If you disappeared right this minute, who do you think would miss you the most?

1271. Which movie can always make you laugh, no matter how often you watch it?

1272. If you had one hour to spend $1,000, what would you spend it on?

1273. What's your go-to style of jeans, and what makes them your favorite?

1274. In what place and situation would passing gas be the absolute most embarrassing?

1275. If you could ban one annoying behavior for a whole day, what would you outlaw?

1276. What's the last thing you did that got your heart racing with excitement or nerves?

1277. If Houdini had lived longer, what daring escape act do you think he would have tried next?

1278. What is something that, no matter how it starts, rarely ends well?

1279. When people get your name wrong, what do they usually call you instead?

1280. What's the most recent funny or clever hashtag you came up with?

1281. If you could name three baby penguins, what names would you choose?

1282. Instead of saying "who's the daddy?" when you win, what fun phrase would you use?

1283. In your opinion, what's a good age for retirement — and why?

1284. What's a food or dish you only enjoy during the winter months?

1285. If you could invent a new scent for a candle, what amazing smell would you create?

1286. If your shoe size grew each time you thought about food today, how big would your shoes be?

1287. What moment recently left you completely without words?

1288. What physical trait catches your eye first when you see someone you find beautiful?

1289. Have you ever realized you were wrong after "winning" an argument? What was the argument?

1290. What creative (but fair) punishment should there be for people who hog the middle lane?

1291. Do you know someone who can move or wiggle their ears? Have you ever tried?

1292. What's something harmless you still refuse to touch without gloves or protection?

1293. What's something surprising or funny you've rediscovered in a coat pocket?

1294. What's the most recent book, movie, show, or product you recommended to a friend?

1295. Which Mr. Men or Little Miss character best matches your personality?

1296. If you had to stick to a set meal schedule, what would be your go-to meal for Wednesdays?

1297. What would be a hilarious or creative twist to traditional chess pieces?

1298. Would you ever walk barefoot over hot coals if it were safe to try?

1299. If you could create a new encyclopedia on any topic, what would you choose?

1300. How many times (if any) did you get detention, and what earned you a spot there?

1301. What's the best song to sing in your head to keep the right beat for CPR?

1302. Do you think loot boxes in video games should be banned for kids? Why or why not?

1303. What's the most memorable or funny thing that's ever happened to you in a fancy restaurant?

1304. Is there any food that, no matter what, you refuse to try?

1305. Have you heard any interesting or surprising stories about things caught on nanny cams?

1306. Adjusting for inflation, how much do you think it would cost to build the Six Million Dollar Man today?

1307. What's the first thing you imagine when you spot a lone shoe abandoned by the roadside?

1308. If your life story were turned into a book, would you write it yourself or hire someone to help?

1309. If you saw someone crying alone in public, how would you respond?

1310. If you witnessed someone stealing something small from a store, would you intervene?

1311. Has someone ever called you their hero? What did you do to earn it?

1312. How do you react when people talk too loudly during a movie at the theater?

1313. If you could write a poem celebrating a food, which delicious dish would you honor?

1314. What's the most recent thing you grabbed that was way too hot to hold?

1315. Which spray-on product (like perfume, deodorant, or cleaner) smells the best to you?

1316. What trend, item, or habit do you think will be banned next — and why?

1317. If you had the chance to completely redesign paper money, what would your new $ bill look like?

1318. If you could spend a day with a Jungle Book character, who would it be?

1319. Whose voice would you love to hear giving you GPS directions?

1320. What subject gave you the toughest time in school? Did you ever fail a class?

1321. How many books would you say you usually read in a year?

1322. If a bank robber had to pick a funny modern-day mask, what should it be?

1323. If you could invent a brand-new ice cream flavor, what would you dream up?

1324. What's something that never feels quite as magical the second time you experience it?

1325. When's the last time you found yourself completely puzzled by something?

1326. In your opinion, what makes a steak absolutely perfect?

1327. If you could rename male and female goats, what fun names would you pick?

1328. What's something truly awful you should never say at a wedding?

1329. If you could invent a new "bag" for a drink or food, what would it be?

1330. What's a piece of good news you've heard lately that made you smile?

1331. If you could add a small improvement to the human body, what would you change?

1332. What's the strangest item you've ever seen used to make music?

1333. Is there a holiday you think could use a modern twist or complete makeover?

1334. If you were guaranteed never to fall, what bold thing would you try?

1335. If you could name a brand-new beauty salon or spa, what creative name would you pick?

1336. What's the worst hair or beauty mistake you've ever had?

1337. Have you ever sung along to "Bohemian Rhapsody" like in Wayne's World — and who were you with?

1338. What's the funniest or most effective home remedy for constipation you've heard about?

1339. Do you think people can truly change, or are they always the same deep down?

1340. What's something you did recently that made you shake your head at yourself?

1341. How do you think your daily life would be different without cell phones?

1342. What's your favorite or most surprising dinosaur fact?

1343. Have you ever gotten sunburned? How bad was it?

1344. How do you handle it when someone stands way too close to you?

1345. If you had to swap fingers with a friend, whose hands would you borrow and why?

1346. What's the most jaw-dropping magic trick you've ever witnessed?

1347. Would your friends say you're the one to call when something urgent happens?

1348. How would your daily life change if you had to use only one arm for a day?

1349. What's the best advice you've heard about aging gracefully — and did you try it?

1350. Does your family have a tradition that's been passed down for years?

1351. What's the most amazing item you've seen created from recycled materials?

1352. Have you ever braved a cold shower — and was it your idea?

1353. What's the first thing you notice that tells you spring is coming?

1354. If your birthday was February 29, when would you celebrate in regular years?

1355. Do you believe professional athletes are overpaid? Which ones stand out to you?

1356. What's the best test score you've ever gotten — and how did it make you feel?

1357. If your magic beans didn't grow a beanstalk, what magical thing would they grow?

1358. What's the longest stretch you've stayed indoors without setting foot outside?

1359. If you could add one meaningful word to the "book of life," what word would you choose?

1360. How do you typically respond when someone asks you for help on the street?

1361. If there isn't already a word for a yawn mixed with a burp, what fun name would you invent?

1362. What's the longest stretch you've stayed awake, and what was the reason?

1363. How many bone names can you actually remember from school or life?

1364. What's something beautiful you notice every single day, no matter what?

1365. When was the last time you really felt the wind rushing through your hair — and where were you?

1366. What's the boldest or funniest color of pants you've ever dared to wear?

1367. If you could fold towels into cool origami shapes, what would you create first?

1368. What's a surprising or fascinating fact you picked up from a documentary?

1369. Where do you look or go when you need fresh inspiration or new ideas?

1370. What's the sweetest or most romantic gesture you've ever experienced?

1371. If you could design a hotel room with any theme, what creative idea would you choose?

1372. When good news comes your way, who's the first person you reach out to?

1373. What's one skill or gift you're genuinely proud of having?

1374. Have you ever rated something zero stars? What was the reason?

1375. In your opinion, what pizza topping is just wrong and should never exist?

1376. Which teacher from your school days challenged you the most — and why?

1377. What's the boldest or riskiest move you've made in your life so far?

1378. Do you ever think about how many times you chew before swallowing?

1379. What's the weirdest or grossest food combination you've seen someone enjoy?

1380. What songs or games do you remember playing during long car rides as a kid?

1381. Have you ever had an idea that seemed brilliant at first but turned into a disaster?

1382. What's something that feels easy to you but others often find difficult?

1383. What's the funniest or wildest story you have involving a bounce house?

1384. Do you believe in UFOs? Have you ever seen anything you couldn't explain?

1385. What's the worst traffic jam you've ever been caught in — and where were you headed?

1386. If your hairstyle could be compared to an animal part, what would it be?

1387. What three words best capture the feeling of being deeply in love?

1388. Can you recall a time when you were the center of attention and wished you weren't?

1389. What's the absolute cutest thing you've ever witnessed?

1390. Do you believe everything happens for a reason? Why or why not?

1391. What fun or outrageous rule would you add to make marathons more exciting to watch?

1392. If you were a legendary cat burglar, what would be your most daring heist?

1393. What's something you recently did that annoys you when you see others doing it?

1394. How often do you check your phone on a typical day — more than you realize?

1395. Which of your gadgets seems to always be hungry for new batteries?

1396. If you had to cook something using only what's in your fridge, what meal could you create?

1397. What new clothing mash-up would you create, and what fun name would you give it?

1398. What small details make you believe life is real and not just a simulation?

1399. Do you believe your thoughts can shape your reality? How so?

1400. Is there something you know is healthy but you'd never do? What is it?

1401. Have you ever trusted a bad feeling — and been proven right?

1402. What's the number one thing that breaks your focus when you're trying to work?

1403. Have you ever felt like you couldn't go back to a place? What happened?

1404. If you could teach a parrot one hilarious or wise thing to say, what would it be?

1405. Do you believe that every bad situation has some good hidden inside it?

1406. What's the funniest thing you accidentally poked your eye with?

1407. When was your last barefoot stroll on a beach or sandy place?

1408. If you could invent a new shape, what would it look like and what fun name would you give it?

1409. Who in your life makes the most noise when they blow their nose?

1410. What fun or bold new challenge would you create to raise money for a good cause?

1411. What small or big thing could happen today to lift your mood even higher?

1412. Which family dessert recipe would you absolutely include in a family recipe book?

1413. What's the most extreme introverted thing you've done to dodge socializing?

1414. Do you think marriage should be like a yearly contract you can renew or cancel?

1415. Which Thomas the Tank Engine character do you think you're most similar to?

1416. Who do you think has the coolest tattoos, and why do you like them?

1417. What's the most unforgettable story you've heard from someone older than you?

1418. Do you prefer to sleep with socks on, or are you a no-socks sleeper?

1419. If you could shape a garden hedge into anything, what would be the funniest design?

1420. In a two-person wheelbarrow race, would you rather be the wheelbarrow or the driver — and why?

1421. What's the strangest or funniest item you've heard of a celebrity signing for a fan?

1422. If you could invent a family board game, what three ideas would you want to test out first?

1423. What random topic recently led you down a deep Wikipedia rabbit hole?

1424. Can you remember your first kiss? Who was it with and where?

1425. What's one bad habit you think would be toughest for you to give up?

1426. What was your favorite sport to play when you were in school?

1427. How often today have you glanced at yourself in the mirror?

1428. If you could only eat cold meals forever, what hot dish would you miss the most?

1429. What's the highest place you've visited, and what was the experience like?

1430. Do you always have a specific routine when you get dressed? What is it?

1431. What do you think is one question humans may never have an answer to?

1432. What's another food whose name doesn't make sense compared to what's inside?

1433. If you had to choose, do you feel more like a Coke person or a Pepsi person — and why?

1434. What's the funniest or craziest thing that ever happened while you were babysitting — or being babysat?

1435. As a kid, did you ever stick something funny in your nose or ear? What was it?

1436. What's something you possess that no amount of money could ever buy?

1437. If you could only keep one TV channel forever, which one would you pick?

1438. What solid-colored animal would look awesome if it had stripes?

1439. Have you ever gotten a haircut inspired by a famous person?

1440. What movie do you think really needs a sequel?

1441. What's the most epic celebration dance you've ever witnessed?

1442. What games did you love on the playground that kids aren't allowed to play anymore?

1443. What's the coolest thing you've ever won in a contest or raffle?

1444. If you had to confess, which of the seven deadly sins sneaks into your life most?

1445. If you had to pretend the Earth was flat, what would your best argument be?

1446. What three words sum up your personal style or vibe?

1447. If you could choose any place for your ashes to be scattered, where would it be?

1448. What's a piece of advice you've received that's truly stuck with you?

1449. Which outfit in your closet would make the worst choice for a hike or outdoor adventure?

1450. Who was the most popular kid at your school, and what made them stand out?

1451. What's the biggest mess you ever made by dropping something?

1452. How many attempts would you realistically give yourself to pass your driving test?

1453. If you had to dance with a celebrity, who would you dread being paired with?

1454. When you hear strange noises at night, what do you imagine they are?

1455. What fun or silly sign could mean "it's officially over" instead of the old saying?

1456. What's something you did recently that made you think, "Why did I do that?" right away?

1457. Is there a social media influencer whose work you really respect? Why?

1458. What's your ultimate topping for a perfect slice of toast?

1459. If you lost your shoes at the pool, what's your first move?

1460. What's the strangest topping you've ever heard someone put on a hot dog?

1461. Have you ever used a wind-up key? What did you wind up?

1462. In your opinion, what's the rarest thing on Earth?

1463. When was the last time you pushed yourself outside your comfort zone?

1464. What's something you would absolutely not want to find forgotten in your pocket?

1465. How many half-finished projects are hanging around your life right now?

1466. In an alternate world, how would Snow White's story be totally different?

1467. Have you ever looked guilty even when you did nothing wrong? What happened?

1468. What's the farthest north and farthest south you've ever traveled?

1469. If you could lower the legal age for one thing, what would it be?

1470. What's something you own that would be even cooler in a different color?

1471. If you could make up a new catchphrase for Greta Thunberg, what would it be?

1472. Which land animal would look the most amazing if it suddenly had wings?

1473. If you were stuck at home forever, what would you miss seeing or doing most?

1474. What instrument do you think makes the most heartbreaking or emotional music?

1475. Tell a time you tried to be silent but made even more noise — what happened?

1476. How many lines or verses of your country's anthem do you know without peeking?

1477. What's your go-to move for quieting down a loud, rowdy group of kids?

1478. Would you raise your kids with the same discipline style your parents used?

1479. What's something funny or embarrassing you did recently and hoped nobody noticed?

1480. If Jack and Jill climbed the hill today, what would they be fetching instead of water?

1481. What facial feature are you most happy with and would never want to alter?

1482. How would your daily life change without any internet access?

1483. What's a food you'd absolutely avoid ordering on a first date?

1484. When was your most recent "top of the world" moment?

1485. What funny animal would make a ridiculous replacement for the Pony Express ponies?

1486. If you had to say goodbye to TV forever, what show would you miss the most?

1487. If you could invent a new Clue character, who would they be and what would they be like?

1488. Have you ever subscribed to a magazine? Which one captured your interest?

1489. Which music album do you love from start to finish without skipping a song?

1490. What slang word do you catch yourself using all the time?

1491. Are you good at recognizing songs just from the first few notes?

1492. What's your best story where something that seemed free definitely came with a hidden cost?

1493. What two totally different animals would make a funny race pair like the tortoise and the hare?

1494. What's one priceless thing you wish you had right now?

1495. If you had a million dollars only for helping others, how would you use it?

1496. When you get first pick from a box of chocolates, which one is your no-brainer choice?

1497. If you had to walk backward all day, which part of your routine would be the hardest?

1498. What funny or random topic would you love to hear Ed Sheeran write a song about?

1499. As a kid, what age seemed ancient to you?

1500. Have you ever saved or rescued an animal? What's the story?

1501. What's your favorite time of day and why?

1502. What three items would you get rid of first if you had to declutter today?

1503. What song keeps looping in your head lately?

1504. Do you believe that remembering others' struggles puts your own in perspective?

1505. What inspirational quote would be perfect for selling shoes?

1506. Tell about a time when you didn't get the joke everyone else found hilarious.

1507. What's the most recent way you gave yourself a little well-deserved treat?

1508. How many times do you usually boil the kettle each day?

1509. What's a harmless but extremely annoying "torture" you think would drive people crazy?

1510. Was there ever a song you loved... until you paid closer attention to the lyrics?

1511. If you could choose anyone famous to mentor you, who would it be and why?

1512. Is there anyone you've held a grudge against for years? Can forgiveness happen?

1513. Is there really an age when you're "too old" to break out some street dance moves?

1514. What old playground game would be hilarious to see as an Olympic event?

1515. Did your grandparents ever tell you a story so wild you weren't sure it was true?

1516. What's the worst kind of music to hear when you're stuck on hold?

1517. Should we stop mass balloon releases to protect the environment?

1518. What's the last GIF you sent or shared, and what made it perfect for the moment?

1519. If you could invent a new cheese with a funny name like "Stinking Bishop," what would you call it?

1520. What is something positive or meaningful that you have now but didn't a year ago?

1521. Do you remember your first attempt at eating with chopsticks? What was it like?

1522. If you could prove one myth wrong forever, which one would it be?

1523. Have you seen someone change for the worse after getting just a little bit of power?

1524. Have you ever found something amazing that someone else threw away?

1525. You're writing a song. What fun or creative rhyme would you use for "She had jet-black hair..."?

1526. What creative punishment would fit for people who litter?

1527. If chewing became impossible, what delicious food would you miss the most?

1528. Who among your friends has the most unforgettable table manners — and why?

1529. Do you know what the most popular baby names were the year you were born?

1530. What do you think would happen if every toilet in the world was flushed at the same time?

1531. If you could have a $500 gift card to any store, which one would you choose?

1532. Who did you last see a movie with at the theater, and what did you watch?

1533. What modern technology do you think will soon disappear?

1534. What's the strangest or coolest plant you've ever learned about?

1535. If a wristwatch could have one awesome extra feature, what would you add?

1536. If you were stuck in an elevator for hours, what food would you hope someone brought you?

1537. In your view, what are three qualities that instantly make someone likable?

1538. If you had $50 to make someone's day better, how would you spend it?

1539. What personal skill would give you the best chance in a zombie apocalypse?

1540. Have you ever done the mannequin challenge, and what pose did you strike?

1541. If humans found something shocking on Mars, what would be the craziest thing?

1542. When was the last time you truly felt you made a positive difference for someone?

1543. What everyday item would feel scary if someone carried it onto a plane?

1544. On a dark, stormy night, would you open the door for an unexpected visitor?

1545. What were the names of your two favorite childhood toys?

1546. What's the most recent thing you downloaded onto your device?

1547. If you had to swap teeth with an animal for a day, which animal would you pick?

1548. What personal action are you proud of for making the world better?

1549. Have you ever cried tears of pure happiness? When and why?

1550. Are you concerned about robots becoming too powerful? Why or why not?

1551. What's the most awesome thing you've ever bought from a dollar store?

1552. Have you ever worn yesterday's underwear to work or school without realizing it?

1553. What's a job that deserves way more respect than it usually gets?

1554. In your opinion, what amount of money would feel like "enough"?

1555. What's the wildest thing you've done when you were really tired?

1556. What's a flavor you can always taste, even if someone tries to hide it?

1557. If you had to make a gluten-free vegan lunch, what would you prepare?

1558. If you invented a man-eating plant, what would you name it?

1559. What small win always feels surprisingly huge to you?

1560. Instead of saying "as old as the hills," what funny comparison would you make?

1561. If you could talk to your ten-year-old self, what advice would you give?

1562. Has anyone ever said you look or act like a celebrity? Who was it?

1563. What's the nastiest or weirdest thing you've ever seen sealed in a jar?

1564. When was the last time someone made you feel like screaming, and why?

1565. Which food would you ban from being eaten in small or crowded places?

1566. Do you believe there's no such thing as a stupid question? Why or why not?

1567. What's something you absolutely love more than cats love sitting in boxes?

1568. Have you ever tried frying an egg on a hot car hood?

1569. What's the smartest lazy solution you've ever witnessed?

1570. If you could choose a different "cloud number" to be on besides Cloud Nine, what would it be and why?

1571. In a parallel universe, what funny or unusual medals would athletes compete for?

1572. Who was the last person you visited in a hospital, and why were they there?

1573. What's the most awe-inspiring natural wonder you've witnessed?

1574. Is there a style of music you find really hard to enjoy?

1575. In your view, what's the most important ingredient for a strong relationship?

1576. Which of your friends is the moodiest, and how do you cheer them up?

1577. How would you solve the problem if endangered animals started eating endangered plants?

1578. You're writing a poem — what would you rhyme with "looking at the sun"?

1579. What's the craziest story you have about terrible neighbors?

1580. If you could only buy one piece of clothing per year, what would you choose?

1581. If you could invent a new potato chip flavor, what would it taste like?

1582. How many bands can you name that have a number in their title?

1583. If you could bury something today just to confuse future archaeologists, what would it be?

1584. Have you ever watched a movie at a drive-in theater? What was it like?

1585. What's something that turned out way harder than you expected?

1586. How big would a lottery win have to be for you to quit working?

1587. Which poem or speech would you love to memorize perfectly?

1588. Where and when did you last watch a fireworks show?

1589. What's the best TV show or movie you stumbled across by accident?

1590. Who in your family knows the most about tea?

1591. What's the weirdest or coolest way you've traveled somewhere?

1592. If you lived during World War I and were drafted, would you have resisted?

1593. What's the funniest or wildest thing you've seen parents do to soothe a baby?

1594. Have you ever called someone by a nickname you later regretted?

1595. What's the softest thing your hands have ever felt?

1596. Who last asked for your help, and what did they need?

1597. What's a food you secretly love but rarely admit to?

1598. How many seconds' head start would you need to outrun Usain Bolt to your bathroom?

1599. What's the most uncomfortable thing you've ever worn just to look good?

1600. Which college major do you think is least practical for getting a job?

1601. What's the weirdest but true excuse you've ever heard for missing something?

1602. If bananas weren't curved, what shape would be fun instead?

1603. What time did you go to bed when you were around ten years old?

1604. How would you spend a Saturday night if there was no power for two hours?

1605. Which past hairstyle makes you laugh or cringe now when you see old photos?

1606. What's your best strategy for taking off a stubborn bandage from your leg?

1607. What recent task did you dread but found surprisingly manageable?

1608. After watching Jaws, were you scared to swim again?

1609. What's one thing about yourself that makes you smile with pride?

1610. If you had just 60 seconds to shower each week, which areas would you wash first?

1611. Who do you know that's infamous for having the smelliest feet?

1612. Did you invent any funny words as a kid because you couldn't pronounce things?

1613. What's a moment you're not proud of but learned a lesson from?

1614. Do you believe that crime is never worth it? Why or why not?

1615. What's the coolest drone photo you've ever come across?

1616. Has someone ever proudly shown you something you found a little creepy? What was it?

1617. If you could invent a new color for toilet paper, what would it be?

1618. When was the last time you felt unusually lucky?

1619. What's the coolest balloon creation you've ever seen?

1620. If you had to wear giant clown shoes all day, what would be the hardest thing to do?

1621. What useful tool would you invent to add to a Swiss army knife?

1622. If lentils had to be the star of your meal, what dish would you create?

1623. What's your favorite knock-knock joke you love to tell?

1624. If your workplace hosted a fun Olympics, what unusual events would you create?

1625. What's the quote that lifts you up when you need motivation?

1626. Do you believe everyone should automatically be an organ donor unless they opt out?

1627. What's the earliest you've ever secured tickets for an event you were excited about?

1628. Which cartoon reboot from your childhood missed the mark for you?

1629. What's the wildest or most hilarious rumor you've heard about yourself?

1630. If you had a pet dragon, what strong or silly name would you give it?

1631. What's one habit or mindset you'd like to work on to become your best self?

1632. How much would your life change if you decided to stop traveling by plane?

1633. If you could invent a Hall of Fame, what would it honor and who gets in first?

1634. Beyond diamonds, what do you think truly brings value or joy to someone's life?

1635. What witty comeback or clever response do you remember most?

1636. If you could turn a wall into a quirky tourist attraction, what would people stick to it?

1637. When was the last time someone gave you advice you didn't take—how did it turn out?

1638. When did someone really test your patience—how did you handle it?

1639. If you had to express your personality through a daily headpiece, what would you wear?

1640. What's the most ambitious thing you've ever built with your hands just for fun?

1641. Imagine a story where bugs take charge—what's your book called and what's the plot?

1642. Who in your life has a signature sneeze you can hear from a mile away?

1643. How many music groups can you name that include a color in their name?

1644. If you could add one new character to a classic animated toy cast, who would it be and why?

1645. If you could switch your way of speaking for a week, which regional or global accent would you try on?

1646. What belief or habit have you stopped resisting and come to embrace over time?

1647. If asked to handle an emergency landing with only voice instructions, how calm do you think you'd stay?

1648. What would you call a cover band that pays homage to your all-time favorite artist?

1649. Was there ever a moment in your education when a small reward felt like a big win?

1650. What food would you happily avoid forever if it suddenly became bad for your health?

1651. If your wardrobe had to revolve around just one T-shirt color, which would you pick and why?

1652. What's something seemingly small that recently sent you into a passionate monologue?

1653. Have you ever nurtured a plant from seed to sprout—and what did it teach you?

1654. What's something in your town that locals take for granted but travelers come to see?

1655. What's one piece of skin-care wisdom you wish you knew as a teenager?

1656. Which jelly bean flavor brings back memories or makes you smile every time?

1657. If money weren't made of paper, what fun or unusual material could it be printed on?

1658. What's something you've collected over the years, and what drew you to it?

1659. What food just isn't complete without a pinch of salt?

1660. When was the last time you had a real conversation on a landline phone?

1661. What's one food that you unapologetically drench in ketchup every time?

1662. If your life were a movie, who would walk beside you in the closing scene?

1663. What's the most bizarre place a fictional villain might hide their secrets?

1664. What's something in your town that locals take for granted but travelers come to see?

1665. What's one piece of skin-care wisdom you wish you knew as a teenager?

1666. Which jelly bean flavor brings back memories or makes you smile every time?

1667. If money weren't made of paper, what fun or unusual material could it be printed on?

1668. What's something you've collected over the years, and what drew you to it?

1669. What food just isn't complete without a pinch of salt?

1670. When was the last time you had a real conversation on a landline phone?

1671. What's one food that you unapologetically drench in ketchup every time?

1672. If your life were a movie, who would walk beside you in the closing scene?

1673. What's the most bizarre place a fictional villain might hide their secrets?

1674. What simple thing never fails to lift your spirits on a rough day?

1675. If you had to sell something you didn't believe in, what would be your worst pick?

1676. What's a childhood belief you had that now makes you laugh?

1677. What brand do you know that's called something totally different in another country?

1678. When did someone last catch you off guard in the best way possible?

1679. If you had to commit to just one chip flavor forever, which would you choose?

1680. What's the most clever or funny line you've ever seen on a shirt?

1681. Were you (or someone close) ever part of a subculture that changed your style or music?

1682. Which classic storybook or rhyme character reminds you of yourself?

1683. If commuting disappeared and you could teleport, how would your routine change?

1684. What childhood fad did you long to be part of but had to sit out?

1685. If we had to invent a single global word for "pants," what would you call them?

1686. How do you keep your headphones from becoming a tangled mess?

1687. If you could design your own T-shirt slogan, what would it say?

1688. Who in your life always feels worth the time—no matter how busy you are?

1689. If you were an advice columnist, what topics would you feel confident helping people with?

1690. If you could only have one kind of sausage again, which one would win and why?

1691. What was the most recent photo you shared with someone and why did you choose it?

1692. When did you (or someone else) totally crack up the room without even trying?

1693. If you had to leave quickly and could only take one thing, what would you choose?

1694. Have you ever had something personally engraved with your name or initials?

1695. Who did you invite to your first sleepover, and what stands out in your memory?

1696. When did you last find yourself in a massive crowd, and how did it feel?

1697. Do you enjoy switching up your living space? How often do you do it?

1698. Have you ever experienced a dinner gone wrong? What happened and how did you recover?

1699. Who in your life tends to overreact the most—and how do you usually respond?

1700. Which dish do you find overrated because it's too fussy to enjoy?

1701. If you had to invent a funny word for sneezing and passing gas at once, what would it be?

1702. Is there something meaningful or fun you're putting money aside for right now?

1703. When you're having a roast, what sides or extras do you always want on your plate?

1704. Can you think of a time when breaking a rule felt like the right thing to do?

1705. What creative consequence would you give someone who drinks straight from the milk carton?

1706. Think of all the four-member music groups you can—how many come to mind?

1707. What's something you've recently repaired or made work again?

1708. Have you ever had a shiner—accident, sport, or something else?

1709. Which Seinfeld character do you see a little of yourself in, and why?

1710. Do you have a hack for cutting or peeling pineapples without making a mess?

1711. If you owned a boat, what would its name be—and what's the story behind it?

1712. How do you balance honesty and kindness when someone wants your opinion?

1713. What's your go-to toast or phrase when raising your glass with friends?

1714. Can you think of a time when breaking a rule felt like the right thing to do?

1715. What creative consequence would you give someone who drinks straight from the milk carton?

1716. Think of all the four-member music groups you can—how many come to mind?

1717. What's something you've recently repaired or made work again?

1718. Have you ever had a shiner—accident, sport, or something else?

1719. Which Seinfeld character do you see a little of yourself in, and why?

1720. Do you have a hack for cutting or peeling pineapples without making a mess?

1721. If you owned a boat, what would its name be—and what's the story behind it?

1722. How do you balance honesty and kindness when someone wants your opinion?

1723. What's your go-to toast or phrase when raising your glass with friends?

1724. Have you ever participated in a survey that made you pause and wonder if it was real?

1725. Have you ever taken a course online, and what did you learn from it?

1726. How do you craft the perfect cup of hot chocolate?

1727. If you had endless resources and no time limits, what five destinations would you visit first and why?

1728. Is there a musical instrument whose sound you just canâ€™t stand?

1729. If you suddenly appeared six feet to your right, where would you land—and would it be safe?

1730. Do you have any quirky superstitions or lucky habits?

1731. What's a nickname you've had—funny, strange, or meaningful?

1732. What is one moment from this month that lifted your spirits the most?

1733. Can you remember the last person you shared a high-five with, and what was it for?

1734. What would you do if a mysterious package showed up at your door with no name you recognize?

1735. Which dynamic duo always makes you laugh, no matter what?

1736. What's something your parents caught you doing that made you believe they had secret powers?

1737. What three changes would make your life feel more meaningful or joyful right now?

1738. What skill or task are you hilariously terrible at—but kind of proud of anyway?

1739. What makes your space feel like home—and how does it comfort you?

1740. What recent disagreement taught you something about yourself—or others?

1741. If the mic is in your hand and the lights are on, what's your go-to anthem?

1742. Who in your family makes you nervous behind the wheel—and why?

1743. Which chair or seat in your home holds a story, memory, or comfort that's hard to replace?

1744. What comforting food or drink from childhood still brings you a sense of healing?

1745. In a towel emergency, what's your creative solution to drying off with dignity?

1746. What recent coincidence or chance encounter made the world feel tiny?

1747. What quote from a film do you often sneak into everyday conversation?

1748. Have you ever exchanged letters with someone far away—and what did you learn from it?

1749. What's a clever way you've convinced a child or pet to take medicine without a fight?

1750. If something unexpected happened at home, who would notice— and how soon?

1751. Is there a truth you'd rather leave undiscovered—for your own peace of mind?

1752. Has technology helped or hurt the magic of watching sports live?

1753. What practical lesson should be a must-have before graduation?

1754. If you were creating a playful children's story about a brave hen, what would you name her?

1755. What bit of wisdom stuck with you—and found its way into someone else's life?

1756. If you were building a fun version of Stonehenge, what would you use instead of stones?

1757. You're camping deep in the woods—what set of tracks would send chills down your spine?

1758. Imagine founding a country—what quirky or meaningful name would your money have?

1759. What's something you think people need to move on from already?

1760. If someone close to you broke the law, where would you draw the line in protecting them?

1761. When was the last time you challenged someone to a stare-down, and how did it end?

1762. If a new animal were added to the zodiac, which one would fit— and why?

1763. How often do you give your phone a new look with a different case?

1764. What farewell in your life felt the most emotional or unforgettable?

1765. What clothing trend did you immediately realize just wasn't "you"?

1766. What's your go-to trick for getting windows sparkling clean?

1767. If a super-strong glue had to be named after an animal, what would be a fun (or fierce) choice?

1768. Is there a show that still makes you adjust your schedule just to watch it in real time?

1769. Have you ever sworn something would never happen—only to be proven wrong?

1770. Do you know someone who constantly thinks they're sick—and what was their most dramatic worry?

1771. Have you ever passed by a place that gave you major haunted-house vibes?

1772. What playful sound would make police sirens less stressful—just for one day?

1773. What hobby or passion excites you—even if your friends just don't get it?

1774. Have you worked with a personal trainer before? What would you want to focus on most if you did?

1775. If you invented a new juice flavor, what would go into it and what fun name would you give it?

1776. What song perfectly captures your vibe and would make a great intro to your own show?

1777. What images, quotes, or people were on your walls during your teen years?

1778. Do you go in for the squeeze, or do you wait it out like a skincare saint?

1779. What theory do you believe about the mysterious disappearance of this famous aviator?

1780. What combination of silly or expressive features would you wear if your face could swap out like a toy's?

1781. Did you ever master the classic arm-sound trick—and could you actually hit a rhythm with it?

1782. What small sound, texture, or action gives you that satisfying tingly feeling?

1783. Quick brain game: how many R-animals can you name in a minute?

1784. When you need peace or a mental reset, where do you imagine going?

1785. If you could own one futuristic device from a film, what would it be and how would you use it?

1786. What track would you gladly put on repeat for seven straight days?

1787. What's something recent that made you say "I'm sorry," and how was it received?

1788. Who in your life shares a name with a celebrity—and how do they feel about it?

1789. Is there a dish from your childhood that no restaurant or recipe can match?

1790. When's the last time you let loose in a full-blown pillow battle?

1791. When you picture yourself sprinting, what animal or object matches your speed and style?

1792. If you could rebrand a tech giant like Google with a new motto, what would it say?

1793. Where do you stand on assisted dying—should individuals have the right to choose when to go?

1794. What's a clever, unexpected way a fictional character might commit a crime in a novel you're writing?

1795. What do you believe gives the Mona Lisa that unforgettable, mysterious expression?

1796. Would you ever choose a travel destination completely at random? Why or why not?

1797. Is there a show you secretly enjoy solo—what makes it better alone?

1798. Do you follow a specific system when loading your dishwasher, or does it change each time?

1799. How do you keep the tears away while prepping onions? Any tried-and-true tricks?

1800. If Post-Its disappeared, what small part of your life would get messier or more frustrating?

1801. What was the moment you realized you let someone down, and how did you respond afterward?

1802. If you could tour any place in the world with a guide, where would you go and why?

1803. What is something you'd refuse to do, no matter how big the reward?

1804. If you had second thoughts about a huge life decision, what would help you feel grounded again?

1805. What's the most curious pre-game ritual or sports superstition you've come across?

1806. Do you believe treasure found by chance should belong to the finder or be shared?

1807. What is one life lesson you only understood after experiencing it yourself?

1808. Do you think your everyday life has more opportunity than your parents' generation?

1809. What playful or silly name would you give to a fictional driving school?

1810. What single word would you use to express yourself all day if that was your only option?

1811. Have you ever felt like you had a unique insight, only to later realize it was common knowledge?

1812. What's the most unusual museum you've ever come across, and what was it about?

1813. What film score gave you chills long after the movie ended?

1814. If you could invent a wacky disguise for a singing show, what would it look like?

1815. Can you recall a time when a surprise totally shifted your day?

1816. Is there a number you naturally choose when asked to pick between one and ten? Why that one?

1817. Do novelty car accessories like fake lashes amuse or annoy you?

1818. Do you believe life starts anew at forty, or does it just shift gears?

1819. Can you recall something you started and then decided to walk away from? Why?

1820. When did you last choose a call over a text, and why?

1821. If you were to rename the iconic six characters from Friends, what names would you choose to reflect today's world?

1822. Picture a giant animal shrunken to mouse-size—what would be the most adorable miniature version?

1823. Have you ever had to deal with a tick? How did you handle it, and what did you learn?

1824. What mysterious ingredient do you imagine gives Coke its unique taste?

1825. Who in your life has the longest or most elaborate name you've ever heard?

1826. Is there a favorite song of yours that lost its magic after being overplayed in ads?

1827. What trends or habits defined the "cool crowd" when you were growing up?

1828. Do you treat your bucket list like a growing document—adding more as you go?

1829. Have you ever thought about where your stuff should go after you're gone—and why?

1830. Think back—has a wish you made ever come true? What happened?

1831. If you could plan the perfect romantic getaway now, where would you go?

1832. What's a lesser-known fact about you that might surprise even your friends?

1833. If your personality was one of many layers, which would you want people to see first—and why?

1834. In your opinion, what three animals win the gold medal for cuteness—and why?

1835. When the music plays, do you sing along like nobody's watching—or keep it in your head?

1836. What popular TV show just doesn't live up to the hype, in your opinion?

1837. If you needed to protect yourself in a pinch, what would you instinctively reach for at home?

1838. Imagine blending three instruments into one brand new sound— what would you create and name it?

1839. What's one decision or experience that taught you a big lesson— and what would you warn others about?

1840. What's the most confusing, funny, or bizarre road sign you've come across while traveling?

1841. Did you ever have an imaginary companion growing up—and if you invented one now, what would they be like?

1842. What's a small but amazing discovery you've made lately that others would benefit from too?

1843. Who recently tested your patience or unexpectedly threw off your mood—and what happened?

1844. If you had to suddenly develop a dangerous allergy, which one would feel the most difficult to live with?

1845. If you had to spend your birthday solo this year, how would you choose to honor yourself?

1846. If you could remix the classic song with a brand-new animal and noise, what would you choose?

1847. If we reimagined the look of crosswalks, what bold or creative color scheme should take over?

1848. What is something you know—without a doubt—you'll never buy, no matter what?

1849. Thinking back, how many different homes or places have you called your address so far?

1850. Which film remake just didn't live up to the original and should have been left alone?

1851. If your world had to be in grayscale except for one color, which hue would you choose to keep?

1852. What unexpected thing pulled you away from your workday or routine recently?

1853. Who in your life still treats a smartphone like a mystery device?

1854. Which sound instantly triggers a sense of sorrow or loss in you?

1855. If the sky had to be a new color forever, what would you want to look up and see?

1856. Imagine you're The Thinker statue for a day—what would your deepest thought be?

1857. Do you regularly switch up your digital wallpaper—or are you loyal to one favorite image?

1858. What do you love most about your town or neighborhood—and why do those things matter to you?

1859. When a fly buzzes in your space, do you trap it, release it, or ignore it?

1860. What roommate behaviors would instantly become deal-breakers for you?

1861. If you had your own island, what would you name it to reflect your personality?

1862. When someone asks "How are you?", what do you usually say without even thinking?

1863. Growing up, was there a space where you were sent to cool down? How often did you land there?

1864. What once-popular kitchen tool has completely disappeared from your life?

1865. What's the last TV series you couldn't stop watching once you started?

1866. If you had to guess, what mysterious treasure—or secret—might be hidden beneath Oak Island?

1867. When you meet someone new, does friendship come naturally—or does it take effort?

1868. What's the most bizarre or unexpected thing you've ever seen that you could actually purchase?

1869. What device died on you at the worst possible moment, and what happened next?

1870. What recent comment, headline, or situation made you think, "Seriously?"

1871. If you could rewrite the ending of one major historical event, which would you choose and why?

1872. What athletic trend or gear from the past makes you cringe—and you hope stays there?

1873. If someone could see your personality as colors, which ones would show up most?

1874. If you had a huge group of cats, would you give them all the same name or get creative?

1875. What's a luxury item or extravagant gadget that screams "more money than sense"?

1876. Have you ever had a wedgie prank pulled on you? Who did it and how did you react?

1877. Are you quick to make assumptions, or do you take your time before forming opinions?

1878. Which action movie would sound hilarious if "die" in the title became "dance"?

1879. If you got snowed in while driving, what would be your first move to stay safe?

1880. Which six celebrities or historical figures would be awkward or dull at a dinner party?

1881. If honesty was your only option all day, is there someone you'd try not to run into?

1882. If you could design a new pasta shape, what would it look like and be called?

1883. What was a moment you had to own up to being wrong, and how did it feel?

1884. Fast-forward to the future—what do you think the population of Earth might be?

1885. What fun or quirky giant object would you turn into a hotel or shop if you could?

1886. Which theme song still pops into your head from your childhood or teen years?

1887. When you get truly upset, what does that look like for you?

1888. Is there an old-time job that's gone today, but you'd be curious to experience?

1889. How would you cope if you had to climb 100 flights of stairs to get to work all week?

1890. If you had to pick a tail—like an animal—what kind would you want and why?

1891. If you had to rename a famous cartoon fish, what playful name would you choose?

1892. Do you believe video surveillance in classrooms improves safety or invades privacy?

1893. In what ways has technology made life easier—and more stressful—at the same time?

1894. Who in your family feels like your emotional anchor, and has that changed over time?

1895. What's the most frustrating thing about being sick that no one talks about?

1896. If you could win a music award for your personal style, what kind of music would it honor?

1897. Which film is so cheesy or over-the-top that it became a guilty pleasure for you?

1898. What emotional wounds do you feel time alone can't repair without effort or closure?

1899. If you could add your own verse to a classic kids' song, what would it be?

1900. When you imagine the future, where does your heart picture you living and why?

1901. Which fruit-flavored food tastes the most unlike the actual fruit, in your opinion?

1902. How close are you to getting your five servings of fruits and veggies each day—and what's your trick?

1903. What's one daily action you've taken seriously to help protect the planet?

1904. If you could guess, where would you love to see a surprise Banksy mural appear?

1905. Who in your life or in the world have you admired so deeply that you felt like their biggest fan?

1906. What's your personal theory on the eerie mystery of the Mary Celeste and its vanished crew?

1907. What would your celebrity name be if it combined your first pet's name with your last name?

1908. What fruit do you instinctively reach for first—and is it comfort, habit, or flavor?

1909. When life gets full, how do you decide what takes priority—love or ambition?

1910. What's the most unexpected or hilarious thing that ever brought traffic to a standstill in your experience?

1911. If schools focused on just three core subjects, which ones would you choose and why?

1912. Which item in your home carries deep personal value and would be heartbreaking to lose?

1913. How do conversations about death unfold in your family—open, avoided, or somewhere in between?

1914. What skill or trick did you recently teach yourself using a video tutorial?

1915. What's your personal rule for how often your favorite pair of jeans gets a wash?

1916. Where do you draw the ethical line when it comes to using animals for scientific progress?

1917. If you could invent a quirky or meaningful international day, what would it celebrate?

1918. Does your zodiac sign line up with your personality or do you think it's just coincidence?

1919. What would you build, grow, or protect if you suddenly owned a vast piece of land?

1920. What appliance or tool in your kitchen was a great idea in theory but collects dust now?

1921. Is there a character from a book, movie, or show you once imagined building a life with?

1922. What's your best guess about what lies beyond the event horizon of a black hole?

1923. What symbols and colors would capture the values of a nation you created from scratch?

1924. In your opinion, what's the most unpleasant or thankless job someone could have—and why?

1925. When's the last time you ran after something caught by the wind—and did you catch it?

1926. Which creature's innocent face hides a surprisingly dangerous nature?

1927. If you were stranded in a bathroom with no toilet paper, what would be your backup plan?

1928. Who has made you laugh harder than anyone else, and what makes their humor stand out?

1929. What's a line you know you'll never cross in your life, no matter what?

1930. What song would fire you up and strike fear into your opponent as you step into the ring?

1931. How do you usually eat spaghetti—neatly or with a bit of a mess?

1932. What skill do you have that you never asked for and don't really enjoy?

1933. How do you feel about facial recognition being used in public and educational spaces?

1934. Can you remember your first or most memorable horseback riding experience?

1935. If you had to join a pirate crew, what would you call yourself?

1936. How do you keep yourself entertained during a long airport layover?

1937. If you could rewrite a fairy tale, what scary animal would you pick instead of a wolf?

1938. What types of posts or content do you feel most drawn to share online?

1939. Do you believe that something can be true even without proof—or does truth require evidence?

1940. What's a fun or strange material you'd love to see a house built from?

1941. What's your most vivid memory of feeling freezing cold—where were you and what made it so memorable?

1942. Have you ever watched a friend eat something in a way that made you cringe—like how they handle a KitKat?

1943. If you could only watch one show forever, which one would drive you crazy the quickest?

1944. In what ways do you reflect—or break—the stereotypes people have about where you're from?

1945. Do you have a favorite type of headphones or earphones, and what makes them work best for you?

1946. Have you experienced an unexpected evacuation, and how did you react at the time?

1947. What special place from childhood still lives in your memory, and have you been back?

1948. If you could recycle anything—not just bottles or paper—what would it be and why?

1949. What local kindness project would you start to help people or the planet where you live?

1950. What funny or meaningful word have you invented or heard that deserves a place in the dictionary?

1951. Can you recall a moment when simplicity turned out to be more powerful than excess?

1952. If you could meet and shake hands with any historical figure, who would it be and what would you say?

1953. If you had to choose boots that reflected your personality, what would they look like?

1954. Can you remember a time you had to retrieve something important from the garbage?

1955. What's a small habit or routine you do differently that makes people notice or laugh?

1956. What part of pre-internet life feels totally unfamiliar or hard to picture now?

1957. If you had to describe your height using a fun or unusual comparison, what would it be?

1958. Think of someone else who had a great week—who comes to mind and why?

1959. Which celebrity do you think gets the most over-the-top or embarrassing fans?

1960. Is there a certain seat or space where you feel most comfortable when catching up with friends? Why do you think that is?

1961. If consequences were removed for a moment, is there something you'd be curious to do—even if it's against the rules?

1962. Can you remember the last time a musical number got stuck in your head? What were you doing when you started singing it?

1963. How do you find time to reconnect with the natural world, and what does it do for your peace of mind?

1964. Is there a type of food you feel shouldn't be eaten while walking through public spaces? Why?

1965. Imagine you're branding your own product—what bold or unexpected design choice would make it stand out?

1966. Can you recall a time you dodged a task with a clever excuse? What were you trying to avoid?

1967. Have you ever been in a situation where first aid knowledge was essential? Would you know what to do?

1968. What's been taking up the most space in your thoughts today, and why?

1969. If you could bring one piece of art into your home forever, what would it be and why does it speak to you?

1970. Which series ended in a way that left you feeling let down or unresolved?

1971. If you had a one-word stage name like Beyoncé or Adele, what would it be and what vibe would it give?

1972. In your opinion, what discovery or invention might dramatically change the world in the next decade?

1973. Which actor, artist, or leader do you feel deserves more recognition for inspiring others?

1974. Why do you think some people find it difficult to apologize, even when they're clearly in the wrong?

1975. Can you describe the most beautiful sunset you've ever witnessed and how it made you feel?

1976. What's a small habit you could shift that would create a big impact on your finances over time?

1977. If you could return as an object with a purpose or presence, what would it be and why?

1978. What part of your culture or national history do you hope future generations will still celebrate?

1979. Describe a moment when time slipped away because you were so absorbed in something. What was it?

1980. What habits or parenting styles do you think can unintentionally harm a child's confidence or growth?

1981. If you had to create a fun, quirky store-brand name for something like Pop-Tarts, what would it be?

1982. Looking back over the last 60 minutes, is there anything you'd do differently if you had a reset button?

1983. Imagine Tom Hanks and Ozzy show up together at your place— what surprising reason might they have?

1984. How confident do you feel solving math problems in your head— like at restaurants or budgeting on the go?

1985. How do you view the idea of arranged marriages—do they reflect culture, control, love, or something else?

1986. In a survival situation, how far would you go to stay alive—even if it meant breaking taboos?

1987. What passion or trend defined your teen years but faded as you grew up?

1988. Was there ever a moment when you had to send food back at a restaurant, and how did that feel?

1989. If Gorilla Glue is super strong, what would you call something that falls apart easily?

1990. If you could dream up your own version of Candyland, what would the trees be made from?

1991. What's the farthest you've ever traveled from your home—and what memory from there stuck with you?

1992. Do you ever listen to classical music? If so, who do you find yourself drawn to most?

1993. What kind of invention do you think will come after smartphones—and how will it change everyday life?

1994. Do you think having a class pet helps kids learn responsibility and empathy—or is it too much work?

1995. If you could capture and save one feeling, moment, or memory in a bottle, what would it be?

1996. Have you ever had too much of something wonderful—where it actually lost its magic?

1997. What's the strangest or most unexpected thing you've seen someone transport on a truck or trailer?

1998. If you had to take one color out of the rainbow, which would you choose—and why?

1999. When people wear sunglasses indoors, do you see it as stylish, odd, or something else?

2000. What's the most memorable outfit you've ever had to wear for school or work, and how did it make you feel?

2001. What's the strangest flavor clash you've ever experienced?

2002. If you could be the very best at one thing, what would you choose—and why?

2003. Which app gets most of your attention, and what does that say about what matters to you right now?

2004. Who inspires you as the most impactful human in history—and what makes them stand out to you?

2005. If you had to wear a hat every day, what kind would match your personality?

2006. If you could name a racehorse anything, what bold or funny name would you pick?

2007. What's something harmlessly puzzling you could say that would totally baffle someone?

2008. If money weren't an issue, what kind of car would you love to drive—and why?

2009. Your pies have gone viral—what's the surprising or sentimental secret ingredient behind their fame?

2010. If you could cast the next James Bond, who would you choose and why?

2011. What name would you give to a never-before-seen alien—and what's its personality like?

2012. Have you ever been misunderstood? What did people assume that just wasn't true?

2013. Everyone has a method—what's yours when it comes to eating an Oreo or similar treat?

2014. If you could sit in on a live show taping, which one would you be excited to witness?

2015. What's the most recent bus ride you took—and did you have any surprising conversations?

2016. If you could invent a brand-new Jell-O flavor, what would it be—and why that one?

2017. What's a secret you've quietly kept that someone doesn't know you've discovered?

2018. If you could write a book that changes lives, what would its title or theme be?

2019. Do you tend to trust your instincts—and how often do they lead you in the right direction?

2020. What's something you do that might make people wonder if you've lost the plot—just a little?

2021. Without your phone, which numbers do you still remember from memory?

2022. Is there anything your friends tease you for being "too picky" or "fancy" about?

2023. Do you remember the last time you got turned around and asked for help finding your way?

2024. What's one cliché about your country or culture that just doesn't reflect reality?

2025. If you had zero fear, what famous place would you leap off for a once-in-a-lifetime thrill?

2026. What simple joy or bold experience would you love to include in every single day?

2027. Has a brain teaser or logic puzzle ever completely stumped—or delighted—you?

2028. What piece of fashion would you never, ever wear—no matter what the trend?

2029. If you had to choose a piercing (no exceptions!), what would feel the most "you"?

2030. If you traded lives with your pet for one day, how do you think you'd feel and what would you do?

2031. What product ads have made you laugh or scratch your head because they were just so odd?

2032. Can you recall a recent moment where your reaction might've been bigger than the situation?

2033. Can you list as many 2000s-era music stars as possible—go on, impress yourself!

2034. If you had to define your life's mission in one sentence, what would it be?

2035. Strange scenario: if one organ had to be worn outside your body (and still work), which would you choose—and why?

2036. Is there a live performance you've always wanted to see on stage—musical, drama, or something else?

2037. What's your honest take on cosmetic surgery—for yourself or in general?

2038. What's a small inconvenience that really shouldn't bother you—but somehow still does?

2039. When was the last time you challenged yourself to do something new, awkward, or bold?

2040. If you could cook in any kitchen from a TV show, which one would make you feel most at home?

2041. What kind of tree would you plant if you had the space—one with meaning, beauty, or tasty fruit?

2042. Think back—when did you take a leap of courage, even when it felt scary?

2043. Do you have a unique mark on your skin that's part of your story or memory?

2044. What's a food combo you've heard of during pregnancy that made you go, "Really?"

2045. If you got the chance to sit behind the drums in any band—past or present—which would you join?

2046. What's something you often delay doing, even though you know it's important?

2047. If you could speak a made-up language from any book, show, or movie, which one would be fun to learn?

2048. Is there a clever invention you admire and secretly wish had been your idea?

2049. What scent brings comfort or memories that you'd truly miss if you could never smell again?

2050. Who in the public eye feels like your total opposite in values, personality, or energy?

2051. When people guess your age, do they usually get it right? How does that make you feel?

2052. In your opinion, which sport demands the most physical and mental stamina?

2053. If you could rename a classic storybook character like Peter Rabbit, what name might you give him?

2054. What note, photo, or magnet made it onto your fridge recently, and why?

2055. Did your first car have a name or personality? What name would have fit it best?

2056. What type of email shows up in your junk folder far more than you'd like?

2057. Where did your most recent family getaway take you, and what stood out about it?

2058. What profession fascinates you, even if you know it's not your strong suit?

2059. You've got your own talk show—who do you invite for the very first episode and why?

2060. If your front door could announce your personality with a sound, what would it be and why?

2061. Looking back on today, is there a moment you wish you'd handled differently—and what would you change?

2062. What small thing consistently irritates you more than it probably should—and why do you think that is?

2063. If you could step into a costume from any book today, who would you be and why?

2064. When you find a place with an echo, what words or feelings come out first—and why those?

2065. When was the last time you changed a lightbulb, and does doing small repairs make you feel accomplished or annoyed?

2066. In your view, what's one of the most striking differences between life in North America and the UK?

2067. If a peaceful alien landed in front of you today, what would be the very first thing you'd say?

2068. If safety had a signature sound, what alert would you invent for backing-up trucks that everyone would notice?

2069. If you could secretly transform into any creature each night, what would you become—and what would you do?

2070. What's something you were really into last year but now feel surprisingly indifferent about?

2071. What's the one forgotten item hiding in your fridge right now—and why haven't you tossed it?

2072. In what situations does your patience disappear quickest, and what does that say about your values or boundaries?

2073. Which current song do you think people will still sing fondly 20 years from now, and why?

2074. Which character's death in a book or movie still lingers with you, and how would you rewrite their story?

2075. Can you recall a time you negotiated for a better deal? What was the outcome and how did it feel?

2076. What's the one weakness or temptation that always seems to throw you off your game?

2077. What's your usual way to mark your country's national holiday, and has it changed over time?

2078. What modern phrase best describes living life at full speed or stretching yourself too thin?

2079. If your personal heroes were carved into a mountain, which four people from your life would you choose and why?

2080. How much choice should students have when it comes to the books they study—and why?

2081. What was your most recent awkward moment—and how did you recover (or not)?

2082. Do you believe opportunities are rare and fleeting—or that they often come back in new forms?

2083. What's your go-to drink at your favorite café, and does it say anything about your mood or style?

2084. If you could bottle and share one type of dream with the world, what would it be—and who would need it most?

2085. When was the last time you spoke words aloud from a book, article, or screen? What prompted it?

2086. If you could start a greeting card business, what quirky or clever name would you give it?

2087. Which athlete do you believe has left the biggest mark on history, and what sets them apart?

2088. What's one of your habits, beliefs, or boundaries that people sometimes misunderstand?

2089. What's a song that instantly lifts your energy and makes you want to move?

2090. Can you recall a recent sandwich or panini that really hit the spot? What was in it?

2091. If you could name a firework that leaves everyone in awe, what creative name would you choose?

2092. If garden gnomes could catch something other than fish, what might it be and why?

2093. If you had a mighty roar, when would you use it to stand up, speak out, or inspire?

2094. What do you appreciate most about growing older—wisdom, peace, or perspective?

2095. When you leave a decision to chance, do you notice patterns in how you choose?

2096. What values, experiences, or relationships shape your idea of a meaningful life?

2097. If you could write about anything, what topic would you share with the world, and what name would you give it?

2098. If you could pick any celebrity as your shopping buddy, who would make it most fun or meaningful?

2099. What's your go-to game day snack, and what's non-negotiable for a great Super Bowl spread?

2100. If you could hold on to just one memory forever, which moment would matter most and why?

2101. When you're unwinding in front of the screen, what food completes the moment?

2102. What job or role do you think deserves more respect than it currently gets?

2103. When you're feeling something deeply, do you tend to show it or keep it in?

2104. What internal words or thoughts have stuck with you today?

2105. If you had to describe tying a shoelace step by step, how would you do it using only your words?

2106. What do you think makes the perfect finishing touch at the top of a Christmas tree?

2107. At what point does something go from "old" to "vintage" in your mind—and what makes it special?

2108. What's a small but reliable thing you do to feel calmer during stressful moments?

2109. Have you ever let loose and howled at the moon—literally or metaphorically?

2110. When were you last stuck somewhere with nothing to do—and how did you get through it?

2111. What experience or emotion feels better than anything else to you—and why?

2112. If you had to give up one letter on your keyboard forever, which would be the least painful loss?

2113. Is there a regular health check-up or screening you secretly avoid?

2114. What was the most recent moment—big or small—that moved you to clap out loud?

2115. Aside from using them as money, how else have you repurposed or appreciated pennies?

2116. Do you like to sort things—like pens or crayons—by color, and why do you think that is?

2117. What's the most unusual or unexpected thing you've heard someone tried to steal?

2118. If you woke up as the opposite gender for a day, what would you be curious to experience?

2119. What fun or powerful new name could you create by mixing two famous names?

2120. What subject challenged you most in school, and how did it affect your confidence or growth?

2121. What's a question you'd rather avoid because it makes you feel vulnerable or misunderstood?

2122. What's the most breathtaking waterfall you've seen in real life, and what do you remember about it?

2123. Which vintage baby name feels too out-of-date to ever make a comeback?

2124. Have you ever had a moment where you checked under the bed out of habit, fear, or curiosity?

2125. Which young animal melts your heart every time you see it?

2126. If you had the power to retire one clothing trend for good, what would it be and why?

2127. If you could replace a car's horn with a funny sound, what would it be?

2128. What age were you when you had a birthday cake that still lives in your memory?

2129. Which famous person do you think might be surprisingly dull when the cameras aren't rolling?

2130. What does it mean to you to really dress up, and when did you last feel like you nailed your look?

2131. Is there a holiday movie that's become a tradition for you, no matter how many times you've seen it?

2132. What's one task or goal you've set for yourself today that matters most?

2133. If you had ultimate karate skills, what unexpected thing would you impressively break in two?

2134. Which instrument do you think instantly makes someone look or feel cooler when they play it?

2135. When was the last time something or someone made you feel small or unsure of yourself?

2136. Have you ever had a painful surprise while eating, like cracking a tooth? What caused it?

2137. What faraway or unique place do you think would make for a wild and unforgettable childhood?

2138. Is there a word people often say wrong that makes you smile or squirm?

2139. If you could remove and reattach a body part without harm, which would you pick and why?

2140. If you were in serious need, could you imagine giving up something vital for financial help?

2141. If your personality could represent a brand, what kind of company would you proudly be the face of?

2142. What's the one thing your hometown is known for, whether proudly or humorously?

2143. If you were forming a chart-topping boy band, what bold name would you give them?

2144. At what age do you think people are most ready—emotionally and mentally—to commit to marriage?

2145. Can you recall a time when your planning backfired because the timing was off?

2146. What's a popular movie you've never watched, even though everyone talks about it?

2147. If animals named people, what names would top their list for owners?

2148. What "truth" do you think people might laugh at 50 years from now?

2149. What makes you decide to give up your seat for someone on the bus or train?

2150. What recently surprised you so much that you were left speechless?

2151. Do you eat certain snacks in a quirky or special way—like Twizzlers, for example?

2152. What heartfelt or hopeful message would you send out into the world in a bottle?

2153. What new verse could you invent to add some fun to the "If You're Happy and You Know It" song?

2154. Think about your favorite food—when did you last enjoy it, and what was the moment like?

2155. Imagine you're the lead in a hit show—what kind of sidekick would you have by your side?

2156. Describe your ideal way to spend a calm and happy Sunday afternoon.

2157. Are there certain questions you believe are better left unexplored? Why?

2158. What's a fact or stat you've learned that truly amazed or shocked you?

2159. When did you misjudge someone or something based on looks or first impressions—and how did that change?

2160. Do you have a spot that instantly makes you laugh if someone touches it?

2161. If your town asked you to create a sculpture, what would you design and why?

2162. Are there signs or superstitions you take seriously when something feels off?

2163. Do you know which of the four elements—earth, air, fire, or water—your zodiac sign belongs to, and how does it reflect you?

2164. Has anyone ever ruined a movie's ending for you—one you really wanted to enjoy?

2165. When someone close to you is feeling low, what's your go-to way to cheer them up?

2166. What are two lessons from your mom that have stayed with you through the years?

2167. If you couldn't feed yourself for a week, which food would you absolutely dread someone feeding you?

2168. What's the clean but dramatic word you shout when something painful or clumsy happens?

2169. Who in your life quietly inspires you through their humility and grace?

2170. If you had the power to transform into three forms—anything at all—what would you choose and why?

2171. Which playground games or recess moments do you remember most fondly?

2172. What beach has left a lasting memory for you because of its beauty or atmosphere?

2173. What comes to mind when you think of Switzerland's global reputation—beyond the stereotypes?

2174. Do you think airlines should consider a person's body weight as part of luggage rules? Why or why not?

2175. In your opinion, which villain from a book, movie, or show is the most unforgettable?

2176. What are a few "unspoken rules" people tend to follow without realizing?

2177. If the rain that fell from the sky had a taste, what flavor would you love it to be?

2178. What small change, tool, or habit would lighten your daily load the most right now?

2179. What's something you bought lately but had to take back—and what made you change your mind?

2180. When you pause and close your eyes, what images or memories come into focus?

2181. If we had to reassign meanings to colors, which ones would you pick to represent hot and cold?

2182. What does living an outdoorsy lifestyle look like in your mind—and how close are you to it?

2183. Can you remember when you first tasted coffee, and how did it feel to drink something so "adult"?

2184. What's the most random or hilarious object you've ever found in the wrong spot because you weren't paying attention?

2185. What three personal items would you want buried with you to represent who you are or what you love?

2186. Can you recall a promise you meant to keep but didn't—and how that affected you or someone else?

2187. If you owned a custom picture frame shop, what creative name would you give it?

2188. What situation or person recently triggered your frustration, and how did you handle it?

2189. How comfortable are you with saying no when your values or time are at stake—even if it disappoints others?

2190. What image or moment recently made your stomach turn or made you look away?

2191. If time travel became real—but with a tiny risk—would you go forward or backward, and why?

2192. What childhood injury or accident sticks in your memory, and why do you think it left a mark?

2193. Do you think in today's world everyone gets a brief moment in the spotlight? Why or why not?

2194. When you think of Christmas, what feelings, memories, or values come to mind most strongly?

2195. When do you remember first feeling butterflies for someone, and what made them stand out?

2196. Which retired or legendary artist do you wish you had seen live in concert?

2197. If snow didn't have to be white, what colors would you love to see it fall in—and what mood would each bring?

2198. Which childhood song would totally rock if it was turned into a metal anthem?

2199. Where do you imagine pure happiness lives—whether you've been there or not?

2200. Have you ever taken an unexpected dive—shoes, jeans, all of it? What led up to it?

2201. What odd or unexpected location do you imagine someone learning historic news like JFK's assassination?

2202. Can you say the full woodchuck tongue-twister without messing it up? Bonus if you can say it fast.

2203. Is there something you believe in that others often question, laugh at, or don't understand?

2204. With the power of invisibility for just one hour, how would you use that time—and where would you go?

2205. Which animal at the zoo fascinates you the most, and why do you think that is?

2206. If you had space for just one vegetable in your garden, which would you choose and why?

2207. What personal experience taught you a lesson you carry with you today?

2208. Have you ever knowingly bought a knockoff item? How did it feel—clever, conflicted, or something else?

2209. What song would you jokingly use to signal the night is over?

2210. What aspect of your appearance have you felt self-conscious about, and how has that changed over time?

2211. What baby name trends make you wonder, "Did they think this through?"

2212. What do you usually do to stay entertained when you're stuck in a long queue?

2213. If you had to trust someone else to make every choice for you, who would earn that trust?

2214. Think back to the last wedding you went to—what stood out, and did anything go hilariously wrong?

2215. What activity do you enjoy watching but wouldn't want to try yourself?

2216. Who in your life would cover for you without hesitation if you needed an airtight alibi?

2217. What book do you believe holds timeless value or wisdom that everyone should experience?

2218. Have you ever believed in—or chased—a dream that felt just out of reach?

2219. What's your go-to film when you need a cathartic emotional release?

2220. Which Ninja Turtle do you relate to most—and why?

2221. If a storm suddenly rolled in, where would you instinctively go to feel safe?

2222. Could you ever trade deep emotional connection with a pet for a huge amount of money?

2223. If you could upgrade one part of your body with a high-tech feature, what would it be?

2224. In a moment of desperation, what's the one place you'd hope to land on the other side of chaos?

2225. Do you have a favorite spot to sit in the theater for the perfect movie experience?

2226. Have you ever stepped outside the rules, even just once, and how did it feel?

2227. Is there a specific chocolate that brings back memories or comforts you the most?

2228. With a superhuman sense of smell, what everyday place might become unbearable?

2229. Is there a widely believed myth or pseudo-truth that really tests your patience?

2230. Who has had the greatest impact on the way you live or think?

2231. If the Ninja Turtles were older, what kind of lives do you think they'd lead?

2232. What's the most recent thing you used a stapler for, and why did it matter?

2233. If you could pass on any skill or wisdom, what would you love to teach?

2234. Is there something you wish you had said or done when you had the chance?

2235. What's the most out-there restaurant theme you've ever seen or heard about?

2236. What kind of glasses best show off your personality or vibe?

2237. Can you think of a mix of ingredients—literal or metaphorical—that always leads to trouble?

2238. When you're overwhelmed with digital clutter, how do you prioritize what matters?

2239. What's the most impressive bike stunt or trick you've ever seen or would love to try?

2240. What's a playful or surprising word you've heard someone use to describe being tipsy?

2241. If you could relax on any famous couch from a movie or show, which one would you pick and why?

2242. If you wanted your funeral to include a song that made people smile or laugh, what would it be?

2243. If there were only one last dance left in your life, who would you want to share it with?

2244. After reaching a milestone, do you pause to celebrate or jump straight into the next challenge?

2245. If your phone-checking habit made you smaller each time, what would your height look like by nightfall?

2246. When you run out of the basics in the kitchen, what's your go-to flavor boost?

2247. Who in your life has the quirkiest or boldest style—so much that you'd never ask them what to wear?

2248. Is there a meme that always cracks you up or never gets old?

2249. If you accidentally damaged something a friend lent you, how would you handle the situation?

2250. What do you feel the world—or your world—is missing that you'd love to see more of?

2251. What's the most nostalgic food memory you have from a seasonal tradition?

2252. What local sayings or slang instantly bring you back home when you hear them?

2253. If you had to stash a guilty pleasure somewhere no one would find it, where would it be?

2254. If you could ask only two questions to understand who someone really is, what would they be?

2255. Do you think rare artifacts should belong to museums or private collectors—and why?

2256. How do you define "family" and what makes it feel like home to you?

2257. Who are your closest people outside of work, and how do they shape your daily life?

2258. When someone tells you not to react or look, what do you usually do—and why?

2259. Which creepy-crawly would make you jump the fastest if it landed on your skin?

2260. If you wanted to create a meaningful first impression, where would you take someone on a first date?

2261. Can you think of a film where the lead didn't quite fit—and who would've done it better?

2262. What small or specific thing lifts your spirits every time you see or think of it?

2263. Can you think of a time when experience didn't lead to the best decision?

2264. If faced with a wild animal unexpectedly, how do you think you'd respond in the moment?

2265. Think back to the loudest environment you've experienced—what was going on?

2266. What's your strategy for handling small but fierce challenges—literal or metaphorical?

2267. What's the most clever or funny hiding spot you've ever used—or seen someone use?

2268. What parenting choice or habit did you grow up with that you've chosen to do differently?

2269. When you step outside and take a deep breath, what feelings or memories does that scent bring?

2270. What are your thoughts on hunting endangered or large wild animals—can it ever be justified?

2271. If you could wear a pair of shoes from any film character, which would you pick and why?

2272. Was there ever a time you unintentionally kept something that wasn't yours?

2273. What's a playful or funny way you've heard someone talk about passing gas?

2274. If change were instant, what's one thing you'd shift within yourself—big or small?

2275. Imagine you're winning a trophy for dancing—what style would you be known for?

2276. Can you recall a recent commitment or task that felt like a mistake once you began?

2277. If your movements were suddenly limited to bouncing, what daily task would become hilariously hard?

2278. What everyday service would be way more convenient if you didn't have to leave your car?

2279. Can you remember a moment that had you laughing uncontrollably—so much it surprised you physically?

2280. What would be a fair way to hold pet owners accountable when they don't clean up after their dogs?

2281. If you had to open a locked door in an emergency, which everyday item would you try first?

2282. What's a common stereotype people associate with Australians—and do you think it's fair?

2283. Do you have a special spot for storing personal or important papers—and why did you choose it?

2284. What method works best in your home for dividing up the day-to-day responsibilities?

2285. Is there one cup you always reach for—and what makes it meaningful to you?

2286. Imagine being a pet for 24 hours—who would you choose to belong to, and why?

2287. Have you ever had that sinking feeling when your car ran out of gas? What happened next?

2288. Can you recall a recent moment that made your cheeks turn red from embarrassment or surprise?

2289. What film moment pulls at your heartstrings every single time, no matter how often you watch it?

2290. If you had to paint a picture of an elf with words, what would they be like?

2291. What's an unexpected pair of things that just seem to work perfectly together?

2292. When someone asks about your music taste, how do you describe it—or do you just play a song?

2293. Have you ever reflected on a time when your actions may have hurt someone during your school years?

2294. If you could name a new reindeer on Santa's team, what would you choose and why?

2295. What English word do you find most beautiful in meaning or sound?

2296. Have you ever dropped something into the toilet and had to retrieve it? What happened?

2297. If you could dream up a brand-new candy, what would it look and taste like?

2298. What type of weather brings you the most peace or joy?

2299. What color do you think the ideal piece of toast should be?

2300. What common event in your life would make you rich if you got a dollar each time it happened?

2301. If cost wasn't an issue, would you take a chance on traveling to space?

2302. If happiness had a scent, what would it smell like to you?

2303. If you could make up a mythical meaning for your name, what story would you tell?

2304. What's one indulgence you secretly enjoy, even if it feels a little silly?

2305. Which dog breed always makes you smile with how funny or odd it looks?

2306. What daily task would you love to automate with a hands-free gadget?

2307. Imagine launching a business overnight—what would you want it to do and why?

2308. What delicate object in your home holds meaning, and where does it live?

2309. When you're mid-recipe and missing an ingredient, how do you creatively adapt?

2310. What was the last moment a show, game, or news story got you fired up?

2311. What's your most clever or funny workaround when tools fail you?

2312. Are there any two savory dishes where adding cheese would actually ruin them?

2313. If you could rewrite history, what fascinating thing would you have a famous explorer bring back instead of potatoes?

2314. If you could design the most delightful gingerbread cookie ever, what would its buttons be made from?

2315. If you woke up tomorrow as a world-class athlete, which sport would you dominate—and why?

2316. What's something you bought on a whim that still makes you laugh—or cringe?

2317. If money wasn't a factor, how would you choose to spend your time and energy every day?

2318. Who among your friends or family would be hilariously unhelpful in solving word puzzles?

2319. When's the last time you made or fixed something by hand, even if it wasn't perfect?

2320. What chocolate treat do you always save for last, but still eat when it's all that's left?

2321. Have you ever hidden a key in a super obvious place—and hoped no one would check there?

2322. What trendy phrase or workplace buzzword makes you roll your eyes every time you hear it?

2323. Everyone has their own way—how do you enjoy eating a crème egg, from the first bite to the last?

2324. When someone you care about is overwhelmed, how do you offer comfort without adding pressure?

2325. When building your dream froyo, what topping combo makes you happiest—and why?

2326. What's a funny or vivid way you've heard someone describe being super nervous?

2327. When you imagine the best kind of dream, what's in it—people, places, or something magical?

2328. Who is so important to you that you'd do absolutely anything to protect them?

2329. What modern invention or small joy makes life feel easier or better for you?

2330. If you could creatively rename Star Wars while keeping its spirit, what title would you give it?

2331. What scent immediately takes you back to a craving, a memory, or a meal?

2332. Do you think society judges politicians too harshly—or does criticism come with the territory?

2333. What does a meaningful, everyday life look like in your eyes?

2334. If it meant saving a life, could you confront your deepest fear?

2335. If you were naming a kids' clothing brand, what fun or meaningful name would you choose?

2336. What food makes the loudest crunch or slurp—and do you love or hate it?

2337. If you saw someone in danger, how would you respond—and what would you consider first?

2338. What words best capture that sudden, sharp zing of a brain freeze?

2339. Which animal's mess would you dread dealing with, even if the creature was fascinating?

2340. If you could borrow one X-Men ability, which power would feel most useful in your life?

2341. If faced with a flat tire, are you ready to fix it—or would you call for backup?

2342. When was the last time you held back the full truth, and why did you feel the need to?

2343. If you had your own magazine, what topics would you love to explore each month?

2344. Imagine you discovered a brand-new life form in space—what would you name it and why?

2345. If you switched the function of two everyday things, which would create the most hilarious confusion?

2346. Do you believe order brings peace—or is a little mess part of creativity?

2347. If you had the power to cure one disease, which would you choose to eliminate and why?

2348. When did you last play in the sand like a kid—and how did it feel?

2349. If someone asked what a mushroom feels like in your mouth, what would you say?

2350. In your life right now, how would you personally define success?

2351. If you could speak with a great-grandparent today, what personal or life question would you ask?

2352. When it comes to video game sports, which one keeps you hooked—and why?

2353. Have you ever changed your job title—or avoided mentioning your job—for a specific reason?

2354. Which tiny animal would look incredible (or terrifying) if it grew to the size of an elephant?

2355. Do you remember your last ride on a merry-go-round—did you play it safe or push the limits?

2356. If you had only minutes to get away from flowing lava, what would be your plan?

2357. What's something people love to criticize, but you secretly (or openly) enjoy?

2358. What are the truly priceless things in life that make you feel alive?

2359. What's your personal description of hunger—physically, emotionally, or both?

2360. Have you ever tried—or heard of—a totally odd way to stop hiccups?

2361. What quirky, kind, or creative idea would you love to see become the next big trend?

2362. Can you master Spock's iconic hand sign—and what does it mean to you if you can?

2363. Which insect showing up in large numbers at home would seriously unsettle you?

2364. How do you feel about the way you manage, earn, or spend money?

2365. Imagine needing to blend into your daily life—what colors or patterns would your camouflage have?

2366. If flight became your superpower today, what would be your first destination—and why?

2367. Which Disney tune has lived rent-free in your head the longest—and why do you think that is?

2368. What's your theory about where those mysterious, unmatched socks disappear to?

2369. Ever greeted someone, only to realize they were a complete stranger? How did you recover?

2370. What's something unusual (or oddly satisfying) you've poked your finger into recently?

2371. If two characters from books or movies had a child, who would make the most fascinating combo?

2372. Do you think simplicity is an illusion, or are there still things in life that feel beautifully uncomplicated?

2373. If you could design the perfect one-pot meal, what flavors, textures, or memories would go into it?

2374. Have you ever changed your age for fun, fear, or freedom? What was the story?

2375. Love asks for a lot—but is there one boundary you wouldn't cross, no matter how deep the feelings?

2376. What's the funniest, sweetest, or most unexpected "roses are red" rhyme you've ever heard or made up?

2377. What's a version of "roses are red..." you've heard—or made up— that made you smile or think?

2378. When you open your closet, is there a color that seems to dominate? What does that say about you?

2379. Was there something you wished for year after year, but it never showed up under the tree?

2380. If you had to start a barbecue without matches or a lighter, what creative trick would you try?

2381. Which dog breed do you think wins the crown for looks, charm, or sheer charisma?

2382. What's your go-to system or habit for remembering important tasks or commitments?

2383. If an earthquake shook the ground while you were shopping, what's your first move?

2384. If you could choose a new color for the rainbow, what would it look like and why?

2385. What personal items do you keep within arm's reach while you sleep—and what comfort do they bring?

2386. Can you recall a moment when climbing a tree gave you a new perspective—literally or emotionally?

2387. Who in your life could win an award for the loudest nighttime noises?

2388. When was the last time you played cards, and what do you remember most about that moment?

2389. If Clue came to life, who'd be the smoothest at covering their tracks?

2390. What foods would bring you comfort, joy, or memories if you were savoring one final meal?

2391. Do you think gaining power reveals someone's true self—or changes them completely?

2392. If October had a personality, what photo from your life would match its mood or meaning?

2393. Have you ever "helped" something break because deep down, you didn't want it around anymore?

2394. Which intense or serious story do you think would be hilariously odd as a musical?

2395. What's a fib you told your parents as an adult, and what was your reason?

2396. Which wizard or witch from Harry Potter would make the worst seatmate for a long flight?

2397. What pressures or realities do you believe are hardest for today's youth to navigate?

2398. Have you attended a school reunion, and if so, what emotions or memories did it stir up?

2399. Do you still feel connected to the place you came from—or has "home" changed for you?

2400. When something says "don't touch," do you get more curious—or more cautious?

2401. What's something that keeps your mind awake at night, and how do you usually find calm again?

2402. Which catchy tune or commercial has lived rent-free in your head for years?

2403. If you could step into someone else's shoes—body, mind, and life—for one day, who would you choose and why?

2404. Do you believe greatness is mostly about showing up and putting in the time, or is talent something you're born with?

2405. Are there any color combinations that just don't sit right with your personal style?

2406. What's a skill or talent you've quietly mastered that might surprise people?

2407. Do you think movie theaters should be more like home—cozier, more casual?

2408. What's one mind-blowing truth that still feels impossible to grasp?

2409. Which sound brings you comfort or joy that you'd miss if it disappeared?

2410. What's your personal twist on the phrase "Keep calm and carry on"?

2411. If you had to design a spice rack using only touch and smell, how would you do it?

2412. What's something you saw recently that brought you instant relief or happiness?

2413. If you could magically make one animal disappear from cities, which would it be?

2414. What parts of today's world do you think future generations will miss the most?

2415. Have you ever built a fire in nature—and could you do it again if needed?

2416. What's something in your life you always welcome more of, no matter how much you already have?

2417. Which two animals would sound hilariously wrong if they swapped voices?

2418. Is there a memory you'd erase if you could—something you saw that stuck with you in the wrong way?

2419. If someone had an embarrassing wardrobe issue in public, would you tell them or let it go?

2420. When do you think someone goes from being older to truly feeling "elderly"?

2421. Who's someone in your life whose wisdom you truly admire, and how do you learn from them?

2422. What tiny food do you think should never show up at fancy events again?

2423. Can you recall a night where dancing made time disappear—and what kind of dancing was it?

2424. What's a new dance step you've added to your moves recently?

2425. Imagine the color indigo as a flavor—what would it remind your tastebuds of?

2426. What parts of your work or daily routine make you feel the most fulfilled or energized?

2427. If you were styling a scarecrow for a fun contest, what outfit would you pick to stand out?

2428. Are you someone who packs ahead of time, or do you wait until the last minute before a trip?

2429. How would you describe a meme to someone who's never used the internet—what would you say?

2430. Do you believe that everything comes at a cost—even when it seems free?

2431. Can you recall a recent time you were running behind—what caused the delay?

2432. What's something you couldn't stop thinking about until you finally got to eat it?

2433. If you had the chance to speak to Walt Disney, what would you be most curious to ask?

2434. What's the most unexpected thing you've seen someone try to grill?

2435. If your real life suddenly dropped you into your most recent video game, how would you do?

2436. Do you think we should use science to bring back extinct animals, or should we let the past stay in the past?

2437. When you want comfort or convenience, what kind of takeout food do you turn to first?

2438. Do you believe a person can be born with a dark nature, or is it shaped by life and choices?

2439. Have you ever had a moment where something seemed amazing—almost suspiciously so?

2440. Do you play it safe with your gas tank, or are you the type to risk it till the warning light flashes?

2441. Are there any animated shows from your past—or present—that you still enjoy watching now?

2442. When using tape, do you use scissors—or are you a teeth-ripper?

2443. If we renamed adult body softness with a more loving term, what would you call it?

2444. You've got 60 seconds and a shoebox—what creative or useful thing would you turn it into?

2445. From glazes to gooey fillings, what kind of donut makes your taste buds happiest?

2446. When someone gives you advice you didn't ask for, how do you usually handle it?

2447. If you invented your own word, what would it be and how would people use it?

2448. If one item in your home could talk, what would you ask it—and why?

2449. Have you ever ended up with the unlucky task—and how did you handle it?

2450. What's the most unexpectedly fun or memorable outing you've had recently?

2451. Should kids be protected from head injuries in sports, even if it changes the game?

2452. Is there someone whose constant cheerfulness makes you curious—or maybe a little crazy?

2453. What's a childhood consequence you'll never forget—and did it change how you behaved?

2454. If you had one chance to test-drive any vehicle ever made, which would give you the biggest thrill?

2455. Has the passing of a public figure ever unexpectedly touched you? Who was it and why?

2456. When you face two unknown options, what helps you choose your next step?

2457. Can you think of a creative or funny question where the answer would be "ten"?

2458. If a peaceful plant-eater turned fierce, which animal would be most terrifying?

2459. What was the first book you remember reading cover to cover by yourself?

2460. Whose name from history would you be proud to find on your family tree?

2461. Have you ever written something even you couldn't decipher later? What happened?

2462. If you were in a rock band, what name would capture its spirit and energy?

2463. If you opened your eyes after a ten-year sleep, what would be the first thing you'd need to know?

2464. What's something you think is better left unsearched online?

2465. Can you recall a moment when chewing gum turned into a sticky, hilarious mess?

2466. If Santa's reindeer had games of their own, what would they play—and would Rudolph finally be included?

2467. Look around—what's the nearest round thing, and how might it become your unlikely downfall?

2468. When you need to unwind or challenge your brain, what kind of puzzle do you enjoy most?

2469. Do you look back fondly on the days of flip phones, or are you happy to have moved on?

2470. Which three apps on your phone do you find yourself opening most often—and why?

2471. Can you recall a moment so awkward or embarrassing that you wished you could disappear?

2472. If a truckload of something spilled on the road, what would be the most chaotic or disgusting mess?

2473. If the Hulk had to trade in his signature green, what new color would suit his rage and power?

2474. Imagine a picture that would be nearly impossible to piece together—what is it?

2475. Can you remember a time when you locked something important inside the very thing you needed to open?

2476. Can you recall something you had to wait a long time for—and was it as good as you'd hoped?

2477. What's one simple health or comfort trick that always works for you?

2478. Which childhood cereal brings back memories—and do you still sneak a bowl now and then?

2479. What did your younger self imagine you'd be doing when you grew up?

2480. If creative talent flowed through your hands, what would you make first?

2481. What's something no one can pull off gracefully, no matter how confident they are?

2482. Do you believe in capital punishment—and what values shape your view?

2483. Imagine a silly moment where a villain is caught off guard—what is Blofeld doing when Bond walks in?

2484. Do you believe something awaits us beyond this life—and what gives you that belief?

2485. What small mishap left a mark on you recently—and what were you doing?

2486. When you observe people in public, do you ever wonder about the stories they carry?

2487. If you absolutely needed an excuse, what would your go-to fake illness be?

2488. If you had an elephant trunk for a day, who would be your first (harmless) water target?

2489. Is there a tricky tongue twister you love (or mess up every time)?

2490. What's your take on the idea of facing a fear each day—motivating or overwhelming?

2491. Have you ever seen or heard of an art exhibit that made you laugh, squirm, or totally rethink things?

2492. How would you stay calm and safe if a dog charged toward you during a run?

2493. If you could blend two animals into a fascinating new creature, what would it look and act like?

2494. When did you first feel a strong sense of purpose or clarity about your path in life?

2495. Which personal trait in others tends to push your buttons—and why do you think that is?

2496. Have you ever walked into a room and instantly realized your outfit didn't fit the vibe?

2497. Have you ever had a dream or nightmare that repeats itself—what do you think it means?

2498. What's your least favorite thing to clean or take care of around the house—and why?

2499. When your energy is low, what do you turn to—rest, nature, laughter, or something else?

2500. What TV series do you think deserves way more love than it gets?

2501. Imagine a Monopoly game based on your town—which places would be the "Boardwalk" and "Park Place"?

2502. If people you work or study with had to describe you in just two words, what might they choose?

2503. If your personality were a houseplant, which one would represent your vibe and why?

2504. What shopping trip left you swearing never to return to that store again?

2505. Have you ever had a moment when it felt like your pet truly understood what you were saying?

2506. Was there a place or group you felt uniquely at home in as a kid, and do you miss it now?

2507. What personal techniques help you regain calm when everything feels overwhelming?

2508. Among your friends, who do you think would win a playful apple-throwing challenge—and why?

2509. Which fictional character from your early years felt most like a reflection of you?

2510. What's your best analogy for helping someone new understand American football?

2511. What place do you return to again and again for food—and why?

2512. If you had to drop a rampaging hippo into one moment in history for maximum chaos, what would you choose?

2513. Can you list three Beatles songs in 10 seconds without overthinking?

2514. What's your go-to banana creation when you're craving something simple and satisfying?

2515. Was there a time you bent the rules to win—what happened next?

2516. What daydream recently distracted you so much you forgot what you were supposed to be doing?

2517. If you could redesign the red carpet, what bold or meaningful color would you choose?

2518. What situation would be your absolute worst nightmare to regain consciousness in at the wrong moment?

2519. What color pairings with yellow feel happiest or most stylish to you?

2520. Can you recall a moment when your reflection surprised you— what changed?

2521. Can you describe a moment when even you didn't expect what you were capable of?

2522. Can you recall a time when you were so tired (or bored) that you couldn't stop yawning?

2523. If you could replace your cough with a silly or dramatic sound, what would make people laugh?

2524. Which color just never seems to work for you, no matter how hard you try?

2525. What was the one item in your house as a child that felt completely off-limits?

2526. Whose beauty—inside or out—leaves a lasting impression on you?

2527. Are there roles that naturally suit one gender more than another, or is that just a myth?

2528. What world events were unfolding the same year you arrived— and how do they shape your story?

2529. Which Star Wars costume would you rock at a themed party— classic or unexpected?

2530. Who's a well-known TV host or guest that might be better heard than seen?

2531. Do you untie your shoes every time, or do you just slip them off in a rush?

2532. What's the strangest or funniest name for a food you've ever come across?

2533. If you won a huge prize from a charity, would you give any of it back—or keep it all?

2534. What phrase describes taking the longest, twistiest route somewhere?

2535. Do your daily actions reflect how you hope others will treat you?

2536. Which overused phrase do you wish people would retire?

2537. You're packing light for a short trip—what are your top three must-haves?

2538. Have you ever found a hidden treasure at a garage sale?

2539. What's something about your personality that you're genuinely proud of?

2540. If a national landmark had to get a color makeover, what color would you suggest for the White House?

2541. What's your secret trick for cooling down food that's way too hot to eat politely?

2542. Which emoji do you find yourself using in nearly every conversation?

2543. If Lady Liberty held something other than a torch, what item would make a bold statement?

2544. Which two names instantly make you think of a classic North American character?

2545. What is it about a red button that makes it so tempting to push?

2546. Have you ever tried the challenge of eating a donut without licking your lips?

2547. If humans had whiskers like cats to judge space, how long would yours need to be?

2548. What car brand says "successful" but not "show-off"?

2549. If going back in time meant never returning, would you still take the trip?

2550. What song that includes someone's name always gets stuck in your head?

2551. In what parts of life do you think size really doesn't make a difference?

2552. Which part of your personality feels like it came straight from your family tree?

2553. If a room could tell its secrets, which one would you want to hear from?

2554. What's a recent moment when you acted on impulse and didn't regret it?

2555. What event or plan recently got scrapped, and how did you feel about it?

2556. Do you think competitive video games like Fortnite deserve global events?

2557. What overly sentimental song gets you emotional every single time?

2558. How would you gently approach a colleague about something like bad breath?

2559. What's one everyday behavior or belief we've normalized that really shouldn't be?

2560. If the Earth wasn't round, what other shape would be fun or fascinating?

2561. What daily routine or task do you wish you could skip like hitting "fast-forward"?

2562. If you had space for one comfort item in your pack, what would it be?

2563. What task recently made you think, "Two hands just aren't enough"?

2564. As a kid, what was your earliest theory about where babies came from?

2565. What's the most unbelievable fact or story you've ever read or heard?

2566. What parts of your routine or character would stay the same if you suddenly became rich?

2567. Which groups or clubs have you left behind—and why?

2568. Have you ever walked or talked in your sleep—and what happened?

2569. What dish that's great hot becomes gross if you eat it cold?

2570. What moment in history or your own life felt like the whole world shifted?

2571. When have you agreed to something and instantly regretted it?

2572. What changes do you think evolution will bring to the human race over time?

2573. How far would you go to track down that one missing piece in a collection?

2574. Which brand or company has truly earned your long-term trust, and why?

2575. If you could invest in one company years ago, which one would you pick—and why?

2576. Do you have a set routine when brushing your teeth—or do you just wing it?

2577. Imagine your last wish—you've already used two. What's your third and final one?

2578. Looking back, do you think life has been tougher than average for you?

2579. What's something you absolutely think should only be bought brand new?

2580. When's the last time you joined in a silly group dance—and did it make you smile?

2581. If we had to pick just one pasta shape forever, what would your top choice be?

2582. If your personality could be described as a type of cheese, which would it be and why?

2583. Based on your quirks, what animal might people (jokingly) say you're related to?

2584. If you could appear on any game show, past or present, which one would you pick?

2585. What's your "cherry on top" in life—and is there anything even sweeter?

2586. If you could use one wild invention from cartoons, what would it be and how would you use it?

2587. What's one self-help or personal growth book that made a lasting impact on you?

2588. What children's show do you think was more confusing than helpful?

2589. If you came with a label, what three words would sum you up best?

2590. What kind of wearable gadget do you think we'll all be using in five years?

2591. Could you go a full week without checking your social apps—and what would you do instead?

2592. Who's someone whose story or actions inspire you to be better?

2593. What's something people say early on that makes you think, "We won't click"?

2594. Can you recall a moment when someone's actions completely changed how you saw them?

2595. What value or principle do you hold that's completely non-negotiable?

2596. What's something you swore grown-ups were weird for doing... and now you do it too?

2597. Which brand do you think will be the first to open shop on the moon—and why?

2598. Have you ever tried a bizarre food trend or diet—and how long did it last?

2599. What's the maximum distance you'd travel daily if the role was perfect for you?

2600. Without a ruler nearby, what everyday object could substitute in a pinch?

2601. What was your regular task growing up—and was there any reward for doing it?

2602. If you had to make a bold leap across the Grand Canyon, what wild method would you choose?

2603. What kind of restaurant vibe makes you feel most at ease—cozy, modern, eclectic?

2604. When's the last time you tried limbo—and how far down did you get?

2605. Can you recall a moment when you left a room in anger or frustration?

2606. What's your most frequently Googled spelling word, even as an adult?

2607. What makes you believe (or not believe) in the idea of miracles happening?

2608. What's your go-to word when "awesome" just won't cut it anymore?

2609. What personality traits are the hardest for you to be around?

2610. Imagine your life as a personal brand—what would your motto be?

2611. What modern tool would completely baffle someone from the year 1200?

2612. What kind of restaurant ambiance makes you feel most relaxed or inspired?

2613. What's the most frustrating thing you've ever misplaced, and how did you find it?

2614. If you had to rate your current happiness out of 100, where would you land and why?

2615. What's one personal or professional goal you're committed to achieving, no matter the challenges?

2616. What stories have you heard about what calmed you down as a baby?

2617. Would you wait for someone sprinting to catch the bus—or close the door with a guilty glance?

2618. What futuristic idea seems wild now, but you truly believe will be real one day?

2619. When have you felt totally off your game—and what helped you bounce back?

2620. Which cloud formations make you pause and look up in awe?

2621. What's a meaningful or playful title that would perfectly sum up your life so far?

2622. What's something that's illegal now but you think future generations will look back on with disbelief?

2623. What's your go-to method for making a PB&J sandwich, and why is it sacred to you?

2624. Is there a movie scene with a road trip that made you dream of hitting the road yourself?

2625. When products are equal, what really influences your decision to pick one over the other?

2626. What's the one household object that vanishes regularly and becomes a family mystery?

2627. When was the last time you let yourself fully enjoy a simple moment, like catching snow on your tongue?

2628. What's one piece of home fitness gear you own—and is it used, ignored, or something in between?

2629. How do you feel about making vaccinations mandatory—where do your personal beliefs and public responsibility meet?

2630. Do you remember your most recent birthday wish? Was it lighthearted or something deeply personal?

2631. If you were limited to liquids for a week, which texture, flavor, or food experience would you long for most?

2632. If you had to pick a favorite letter, which one feels most like you— and what does it say about you?

2633. What image, scent, or sound comes to mind first when you think of 'home'?

2634. Which historical or current world leader would be a terrible fit for your country—and what makes you say that?

2635. Do you remember being in a school play or performance? What role did you take on—and how did it feel?

2636. What once-fresh trend do you think lost its charm after everyone jumped on board?

2637. If everything ended tomorrow, would you prefer to know in advance or live your last day in peace?

2638. What's a holiday tradition in your family that brings you the most joy—or perhaps the most laughter?

2639. What's the funniest time you realized you were mismatched—like socks or shoes—and how did it happen?

2640. Can you recall a moment where forgetting something small ended up affecting much more than you expected?

2641. If your head became a billboard, what message or brand would you absolutely say no to promoting?

2642. Are you familiar with the dance moves to 'Baby Shark,' and have you ever joined in for fun or with kids?

2643. What kind of physical movement have you done lately, and how did it make you feel afterward?

2644. If you had to be on a reality show, which one would you pick—and what do you think your role would be?

2645. Is there a song with a day in it that always lifts your mood or brings back memories?

2646. What kind of cake is so rich, sweet, or intense that even two slices would be too much?

2647. Was there a time when someone got blamed for your mistake, and how did it feel afterward?

2648. Have you ever had lice, or heard of a strange way someone tried to get rid of them?

2649. When ordering pizza, do you go for thin, deep dish, stuffed, or something else—and why?

2650. If you could imagine yourself as a butterfly, what colors would your wings have—and what would they say about you?

2651. What's the funniest cat video you've ever seen, and what made it so hilarious?

2652. What other languages can you say 'hello' or 'goodbye' in, and how did you learn them?

2653. Have you ever come across an unusual or downright bizarre piece of taxidermy? What made it stick in your mind?

2654. If you had to write with just one color pen for the rest of your life, what color would you pick and why?

2655. What ordinary activity would become absolutely hilarious if done as slowly as a sloth?

2656. Have you ever been without your voice—what did you do to get your message across?

2657. What kind of natural view makes you feel most at peace—mountains, oceans, forests, or something else?

2658. When you color, do you prefer staying in the lines—or does going outside them feel more like you?

2659. What usually stands out to you the most when you're introduced to someone for the first time?

2660. Who's your go-to person when you need company, comfort, or a familiar presence?

2661. When was the last time you grabbed a pen or pencil and actually wrote something—what was it?

2662. Have you ever helped bury someone (or been buried) in sand as a beach tradition or just for laughs?

2663. If rain could fall in any color for one day, what would you choose—and how would it change the mood?

2664. As you think about aging, what part of it brings up the most fear or hesitation for you?

2665. Which actor would make the most unexpected or hilarious James Bond—and how would it go?

2666. If anime has ever caught your attention, which show pulled you in the most—and why?

2667. Is there a fun or unusual word for money that you like to use or hear?

2668. Have you ever pretended to know or like something just to fit in or impress someone?

2669. What's something imaginative you could build or craft out of old egg cartons?

2670. Do you think people need to see something with their own eyes to truly believe it's real?

2671. Is there a song that you can't help but move to—one where you know every step or motion?

2672. Have you ever jumped around on a big rubber ball with handles—when was your last ride?

2673. If safety weren't a concern, what thrilling or brave thing would you try at least once?

2674. Do you enjoy working out in silence or with sound—and how does that choice affect your focus or energy?

2675. Do you ever feel like things have to be just right—and in what moments does that pressure show up?

2676. If mashed potatoes needed a new name, what silly or fun name would you give them?

2677. Have you ever picked up the phone and faked being someone else, just for fun or to dodge something?

2678. Is there a specific type of snake that makes your skin crawl more than any other?

2679. If you spotted a friend across a noisy room, how would you get their attention without yelling?

2680. What three words would you choose that best capture the spirit or presence of your parents?

2681. What's the longest stretch you've ever spent sitting in a waiting room—and what got you through it?

2682. Is there something common that many people have tried—but you've somehow never done?

2683. If you had to choose the one cake flavor that deserves to be the only one left, what would it be?

2684. What factor would make you walk away from an otherwise great job opportunity?

2685. Can you recall the last time you saw something in a store window and just stopped to admire it?

2686. Is your mealtime routine fixed or flexible—and how does it affect your day?

2687. What feature or part of a park made it the most memorable one you've been to?

2688. If you could nap like a cat anywhere, what cozy or peaceful spot would you choose?

2689. When you think about fear, what comes to mind as the thing that shakes you most deeply?

2690. What's the highest point you'd be willing to climb with no gear—where's your limit?

2691. If you could invent a fun or cute name for baby octopuses, what would you call them?

2692. Can you remember the last time something just clicked—a realization that shifted things for you?

2693. If your dream job didn't work out, what's another path that still excites or inspires you?

2694. In a wild and silly universe, what would replace 'if pigs could fly' as a phrase for the impossible?

2695. Have you ever had to end something with someone—and how did it affect you both?

2696. What fold or style do you use to make a paper airplane that really soars?

2697. Can you do any animal impressions? Which ones come naturally or make people laugh?

2698. What's something in life that still feels strange, no matter how often it happens?

2699. Have you ever tried bungee jumping—or is there a dream location where you'd take the leap?

2700. What's a recent moment where something totally random lined up in a strange or funny way?

2701. Do you remember the most epic Monopoly game you've played—and how long did it last?

2702. If you could sit down with any member of The Beatles, who would you choose and what would you ask?

2703. When did you last get that tingling pins-and-needles feeling, and what caused it?

2704. Is there something you passed up that still lingers in your mind as a missed opportunity?

2705. What's the most out-there, hilarious, or bizarre hat you've ever seen someone wear?

2706. If your footsteps made a sound with every step, what would be the most fun or expressive one?

2707. Is there a time period whose style you'd love to see return—clothing, accessories, or flair?

2708. Do you believe in acting your age, or do you think it's more about how you feel inside?

2709. Is there a shape you find especially pleasing or comforting—visually or symbolically?

2710. When you're in a group setting, do you have a fun trick, talent, or moment that always gets a smile?

2711. Is there a video game with a story so compelling you think it would be perfect for a series?

2712. If you accidentally caused a tiny scrape in a parking lot, would you own up and leave a note?

2713. If you had to invent a playful name for a group of energetic five-year-olds, what would it be?

2714. Who was the last person you wrote a thank-you note or message to—and what inspired it?

2715. Have you ever seen a public figure up close, and did they match your expectations?

2716. What's the most unusual or unexpected combination you've ever put between two slices of bread?

2717. If you had to design a storefront display, what story or feeling would you want to tell with it?

2718. What commercial has stuck in your head over the years—whether it made you laugh, cry, or cringe?

2719. When you're afraid of the dark, what thoughts or images creep into your mind?

2720. Are there any natural or herbal remedies that have earned your trust over the years?

2721. Did you and your childhood friends ever invent a secret code or handshake?

2722. If your favorite remote could have one new button, what would it do?

2723. If there's another version of you somewhere else, what choices or path might they be living?

2724. What modern symbol would you use today instead of 'strong as an ox' to show real strength?

2725. Can you recall a recent moment when your words ran ahead of your brain—and what came out?

2726. Imagine a store that sells nothing but annoyances—what petty or quirky items would be on the shelves?

2727. Have you ever actually met an Aussie named Bruce or Sheila—or is it just a stereotype?

2728. Is there a historical date you learned in school that still stands out in your memory?

2729. When did you last test how long you could hold your breath—and how long did you last?

2730. What's the most difficult or unexpected interview question you've ever faced?

2731. If you came across a bag full of cash on the sidewalk, what would your first move be?

2732. What are a few of your small everyday joys—things that lift you up or make you feel good?

2733. What bumper sticker made you laugh, think, or want to write it down when you saw it?

2734. Have you ever flopped down in the snow to make an angel—and when did you last do it?

2735. Is there a success story that inspires you—someone who started with little and built something great?

2736. If you speak more than one language, which one do your thoughts use the most—and does it change?

2737. If Frodo had a completely different name, what would capture his spirit and role best?

2738. When did you last pull on a pair of rubber boots, and what was the weather or occasion?

2739. If you had to bring a childhood stuffed animal to a picnic, which one would you choose and why?

2740. Which teen slang today makes you pause or feel completely out of the loop?

2741. When food hits the ground, do you follow the 'ten-second rule' or toss it without hesitation?

2742. If you could invent a road sign for modern life, what would it warn or guide drivers about?

2743. If something unexpected landed in your food at a restaurant, would you stay or leave?

2744. Whose voice or laughter carries the farthest in your world—and do you love it or dread it?

2745. If your toaster made a fun or musical sound instead of just a click, what would you want it to be?

2746. Have you ever caught yourself wondering if life had more to offer—what sparked the thought?

2747. If you were a modern-day hero with a cape, what color would express your energy or mission?

2748. What's the most recent word that made you curious enough to check its meaning?

2749. When did you (or when do you imagine you'll) feel ready to leave the family nest?

2750. What's the most recent thing you managed to fix just by powering it off and on again?

2751. Have you ever secretly planned a celebration to surprise someone you care about?

2752. What's something you believe in or value so deeply that you'll never stop fighting for it?

2753. If you were trapped mid-shower and spotted a snake, how would you react—and who would you call for help?

2754. If peanut butter needed a rebrand, what fun or catchy name would you give it?

2755. If you had your own cooking show, what dish would be your proudest creation and why?

2756. If you could witness one extinct creature return to life, which would fascinate you most?

2757. What's the longest flight you've ever taken—and what helped you get through it?

2758. What schoolyard game, toy, or trend ruled your childhood—and did you join in?

2759. If a hidden door appeared in your home, where would you want it to take you?

2760. When you have a choice, do you lean toward comfort and ease—or do you welcome a challenge?

2761. Is there a healthier take on a dish or snack that you actually enjoy more than the original?

2762. In a pinch, what's your most creative fix when your clothes decide to betray you?

2763. Can you remember the last time you jolted awake in the middle of the night—what triggered it?

2764. If Thomas and friends were renamed today, what modern names would reflect their personalities or roles?

2765. Do you remember the first card trick you ever mastered—and who you impressed with it?

2766. How patient are you when a page loads slowly—what's your personal timeout limit?

2767. When you're at an Indian restaurant, what dish do you find hard to resist?

2768. If you spotted a wedding ring lying on the sidewalk, how would you respond?

2769. Do you have a pickled snack that always hits the spot—tangy, crunchy, or classic?

2770. Have you ever helped a friend by watching their pet—and what was the experience like?

2771. If the bend of your arm had its own fun name, what would you call it?

2772. Can you remember the last time you tripped, stumbled, or full-on wiped out?

2773. If you could unlock the truth behind any famous unsolved mystery, which would you pick?

2774. When your mind won't rest, what whimsical or calming thing would you imagine instead of sheep?

2775. If you had to turn heads at a major event, what kind of bold outfit would you wear?

2776. What were you jotting down the last time you made a list—groceries, goals, or something else?

2777. If you uncovered a hidden treasure in your backyard, what would you hope was inside?

2778. Ever wonder why glue doesn't stick inside the bottle—what's your theory?

2779. If you could use both hands equally well, when do you think it would come in handy?

2780. If you had the chance to meet someone from the royal family, who would you choose and why?

2781. What's something you'd proudly add to a list of things you never want to try?

2782. If you had to invent a collective noun for a group of teens, what fun or fitting word would you choose?

2783. Have you ever bought two of the same item but ended up sticking with just one of them?

2784. What was your first "I earned this" purchase—and how did it make you feel?

2785. If intelligent life exists beyond Earth, what do you imagine it would look like?

2786. If you're building a plate at the Pizza Hut salad bar, what do you reach for first?

2787. Have you ever owned a clever gadget like a pen-flashlight combo? What other combos have surprised you?

2788. Have you ever spotted street art that made you stop and stare—in awe or amusement?

2789. Can you do any tricks with a yo-yo—or did you ever try to learn one as a kid?

2790. What's something you gave a solid try—but had to laugh at how badly it went?

2791. Do you have a go-to pose when the camera's out—serious, silly, or signature?

2792. Do you remember your first sip of alcohol—what it was, and how it tasted?

2793. What random or fascinating fact pops into your head right now?

2794. What's something you did as a kid—fearlessly or foolishly—that your adult self wouldn't dare try?

2795. Imagine you're a pro snowboarder—what flashy or wild move would be your signature?

2796. Can you remember the most recent time you witnessed a sunrise—and what the moment meant to you?

2797. Which rock anthem would be surprisingly amazing if harmonized by a barbershop quartet?

2798. Did you ever fill up a piggy bank? What did you use the money for when it was full?

2799. Do you think pretending confidence helps us grow into it—or is authenticity better?

2800. What's the strangest or most unexpected competition you've come across?

2801. When your mind drifted recently, where did it take you—fantasy or future?

2802. Have you ever pulled off an underwater handstand? Do you still try now and then?

2803. If you were a monkey for 24 hours, what part of the experience would you love most?

2804. When did you last feel like you were in trouble—and what was the situation?

2805. Did you ever care for a Tamagotchi—or a digital pet like it?

2806. Do you remember the first time you dropped a swear word around your parents—intentionally or not?

2807. If your life were a storybook, who or what would be your biggest obstacle or antagonist?

2808. Do you have a set routine in the mornings, and how do you feel when it's disrupted?

2809. If you had to leave your neighborhood, what's the one thing you'd miss most deeply?

2810. Do you have a favorite word that reads the same forward and backward?

2811. In your view, is there ever a justified reason for war—or is it always senseless?

2812. If you had to cross the Atlantic in something ridiculous, what would it be?

2813. What fun nickname would you give yourself if you were chatting on a CB radio?

2814. Which online spaces are part of your daily or weekly rhythm?

2815. Are you usually the one who solves the mystery before the big reveal?

2816. What recent act of kindness or courage reminded you of the goodness in people?

2817. If you could create a new Ninja Turtle, what would their name and personality be?

2818. Do you remember the first scary movie that gave you chills—or made you laugh in hindsight?

2819. If cat videos didn't exist, what do you think would take their place as the internet's go-to joy?

2820. If you could live forever, what part of that would feel like a burden or challenge?

2821. Do you look back at your school years as joyful, complicated, or something else?

2822. Do you own something in your wardrobe that hasn't seen the light of day in ages?

2823. If you had to pick a truly dull pet, what would it be—and why?

2824. Who in your life holds the most years—and what have you learned from them?

2825. What timeless style or trend do you think will always have a place in the world?

2826. Have you ever used the classic 'it's not you, it's me'—and did it help or hurt more?

2827. Do you remember the last time you popped in a DVD—what did you watch and why?

2828. If you couldn't bend your knees for a day, what everyday task would suddenly feel impossible?

2829. If a fairy godmother could grant one magical favor, what would you ask for—big or small?

2830. Have you ever faced a moment when no one was going to rescue you—what did you do next?

2831. What's your personal heat limit—when do you officially call it 'too hot to function'?

2832. Back in the day, what was your go-to treat or purchase when you had a few dollars?

2833. Is making your bed a daily habit—or something you skip when time's tight?

2834. If the Hulk had to choose a car, what absurdly tiny or fragile vehicle would he drive?

2835. If you could reinvent toothpaste with a new flavor, what would make brushing more fun?

2836. Have you ever felt disconnected even while surrounded by people—what was that like?

2837. What was your very first cinema experience—and do you still remember how it felt?

2838. Have you ever pitched a tent and spent the night outdoors— where was it?

2839. What song would feel wildly out of place for a romantic wedding first dance?

2840. If your hot air balloon could carry a message across the sky, what would it say or show?

2841. When it comes to orange flavor, what treat or food do you crave the most?

2842. If an emergency arose, do you feel confident enough to step in and do CPR?

2843. What's something new you've tried recently—big or small?

2844. What's the farthest you've ever walked—and what was the reason for it?

2845. What's the dullest event you've sat through—and how did you cope with it?

2846. If someone handled everything for you for one day, what tasks would you gladly hand off?

2847. What non-cash prize would be completely useless—or even annoying—for you to win?

2848. Have you ever quietly messed up something and kept it to yourself—until this moment?

2849. If someone made the world's worst scratch-and-sniff sticker, what smell would it have?

2850. When someone says "don't think of something," does it pop into your mind anyway?

2851. What's something you're genuinely excited about for the day ahead?

2852. Which emoji just doesn't feel like "you"—and why do you skip it?

2853. If there was such a thing as reincarnation, what form would you love to return in?

2854. Who in your family do you stay closest to through regular conversations?

2855. If a chef showed up just for you, what's the first meal you'd ask for?

2856. In your experience, what three traits truly define a great leader?

2857. Is there a mistake you've repeated—and what did it teach you the second time around?

2858. What's the most you've ever paid for sneakers—and was it worth it?

2859. Be honest—how many Pringles do you think your mouth could hold before it's ridiculous?

2860. If Keanu Reeves were cast in your life story, what would his character be like?

2861. Have you ever sworn off a product simply because the ad rubbed you the wrong way?

2862. Is there a hardship so painful or dehumanizing you wouldn't wish it on anyone—not even your enemy?

2863. If you had your own private bunker, what essentials and comforts would you hide away in it?

2864. Do you remember the last time your brain completely blanked the moment you entered a room?

2865. What snack or food would be the absolute disaster to forget about in your pocket?

2866. Is there something you own that's just too personal, fragile, or meaningful to lend out?

2867. If you could make one groundbreaking discovery, what would you want it to be?

2868. If your two favorite desserts were in front of you, what would help you pick just one?

2869. Is there a place on Earth that even your dream job couldn't convince you to move to?

2870. What's one thing—small or profound—you learned today?

2871. If there were no limits, what would your ultimate Lego masterpiece be?

2872. Do you remember the very first joke you learned—what made it stick with you?

2873. Have you ever met someone named Karen who broke the stereotype?

2874. Where do you most enjoy listening to music—Spotify, YouTube, something else?

2875. In a moment of emergency, who's the person you'd want by your side heading to the hospital?

2876. If you had to capture your childhood room in one word, what would it be and why?

2877. Did you ever try raising tadpoles or frogs when you were younger?

2878. What's the strangest group of things you've ever bought at the same time?

2879. What's something you'll almost always say yes to—even when you know you probably shouldn't?

2880. What's something mischievous you got away with back in your childhood days?

2881. In your opinion, what's the exact time for the perfectly boiled egg?

2882. What hands-on skill do you wish you could master for home or personal projects?

2883. If someone in your circle had a hidden identity, who might it be—and why?

2884. Which current fashion trend do you think will seem the most dated in a few years?

2885. When was the last time you got soaked unexpectedly by a downpour?

2886. Which keyboard letters do your fingers seem to hit the most throughout your day?

2887. Is there a performer whose movies rarely land with you—and you've noticed a pattern?

2888. What crossed your mind right after you opened your eyes today?

2889. If you could swap lives for a day with someone close to you, who would it be and why?

2890. If you could design your dream chill-out space, what would it look and feel like?

2891. If you had the guts to join a circus as a juggler, what three unique things would you toss in your routine?

2892. Do you remember the last lightning storm you witnessed—what was the atmosphere like?

2893. If you had to defend yourself during a zombie outbreak, what would be your go-to weapon?

2894. If people remembered you for one defining quality, what would you want that to be?

2895. Do you think humans and dinosaurs could have shared the planet—how would that have worked?

2896. What type of content do you find yourself watching the most on YouTube?

2897. Did you ever listen to music on a cassette Walkman—and what was your favorite tape?

2898. What surprising news or revelation recently caught you completely off guard?

2899. If you moved like a cat—quick, nimble, and smooth—what adventures would you take on?

2900. Was there a hobby or interest your parents thought you'd outgrow—but it's still a big part of you?

2901. Do you feel nervous when speaking in front of a crowd—or is it something you've practiced?

2902. If you could quietly observe life from any rooftop, which one would you choose and why?

2903. Can you recall the last time your body hit its limit and made you throw up?

2904. What simple or special ingredients create the recipe for your ideal day?

2905. If you turned your close friends' names into a band name like ABBA, what would it be?

2906. What dish from Mexican cuisine always brings you comfort, joy, or craving?

2907. If your body were sculptable like Play-Doh, would you change anything—and what would it be?

2908. Can you recall someone whose rudeness shocked or disappointed you—and what they did?

2909. What was the first video game you ever tried—and how did it feel to play it?

2910. If your hair was long and magical like Rapunzel's, what would you do with it?

2911. If you had to swap the egg and spoon for a hilarious race combo, what would you choose?

2912. Have you ever accidentally shrunk your clothes in the wash— what happened?

2913. Can you recall a recent moment when something felt unfair or deceptive?

2914. If you were adopting and two kittens remained, would you still leave one behind?

2915. What strange or mind-blowing coincidence have you come across that stuck with you?

2916. Do you ever pause to read the fine print—or do you usually just hit 'agree'?

2917. If you had to invent a new phrase for the odd one out in a family, what would it be?

2918. Have you ever been caught mid-nose-pick—and what did you do?

2919. If you had to invent a fake animal rug, what animal would it be— and why would it be hilarious?

2920. How long can you keep up rhyming before it gets awkward—or strangely impressive?

2921. If someone picked up a book about your life, what would the back cover promise them?

2922. If the Spice Girls added a new member, what unique 'Spice' name would you give her?

2923. What vegetarian dish do you genuinely enjoy—even if you're not vegetarian?

2924. Have you ever used a disabled spot without permission— intentionally or by mistake?

2925. Which medical diagnosis would frighten or challenge you the most to face?

2926. Would you match your twins' outfits or let their styles be unique from day one?

2927. What new twist, theme, or feature would turn a good roller coaster into an epic one?

2928. What's the most outrageous shortcut you've seen a lazy cook try—like toasting a steak?

2929. Do you remember the last time you skipped the elevator and took the stairs instead?

2930. Are you someone who speaks with clarity and integrity, or do you hold back sometimes?

2931. What quirky or curious idea popped into your head during your last shower?

2932. If you joined a circus, what talent or show would you perform under the spotlight?

2933. Who in your family has the hardest time with phones, apps, or anything tech-related?

2934. Can you recall a time when you knowingly broke a safety rule—big or small?

2935. If you had to give one quirky piece of advice, what material would you say is off-limits for wiping?

2936. Is there any survival scenario extreme enough where cannibalism might cross your mind?

2937. What fear have you outgrown that used to seem huge as a kid?

2938. Have you ever taken a silly or risky chance where the odds weren't in your favor?

2939. What's something people tend to overreact to that's not actually a big deal?

2940. Imagine you're a fancy meal—how would the menu describe your flavor, vibe, or ingredients?

2941. What's the most unpleasant or embarrassing thing you've stepped in and carried with you?

2942. What's the last decision that made you shake your head at yourself?

2943. If you had to carry your essentials hobo-style, what would make the cut?

2944. Is there a specific order or ritual you follow when you shower?

2945. What's the coolest or most intricate ice sculpture you've ever come across?

2946. Is there a word that always trips you up, no matter how many times you try it?

2947. What important choice have you had to make recently—and how did you decide?

2948. What's your usual routine and how long does it take you to get out the door?

2949. What are your must-peel foods—no matter what anyone else does?

2950. If you found a mysterious envelope full of cash on public transport, what would you do?

2951. Have you ever been fooled by something that turned out to be impressively fake?

2952. What's something you waited patiently for—and it turned out to be worth every second?

2953. If your swimsuit vanished in the ocean, what's your next move?

2954. What's the most recent book you finished—and how would you rate it?

2955. Do you remember getting your face painted as a kid—what design stood out the most?

2956. Is there something that's made you feel a little guilty lately?

2957. What's the oldest piece of clothing you still wear—and what's its story?

2958. Have you ever read or heard a heartwarming pet reunion story that stayed with you?

2959. What would be your creative backup if your kitchen had zero mugs for coffee or tea?

2960. What pushed you to your limit recently and made you say, "That's it"?

2961. Do you remember watching a solar eclipse—what was the experience like?

2962. If you walked into your kitchen and saw a raccoon, what would be your first move?

2963. When did you last grab a broom and do a bit of sweeping—what were you cleaning?

2964. If you had to choose one word to sum up your mom, what would it be?

2965. Have your social media habits changed in the last year? What do you use now versus then?

2966. Is there a daily habit you have at home that might seem strange to a guest?

2967. Have you ever texted the wrong person by accident—what did the message say?

2968. If you had to live with a fictional family, which one would drive you the most crazy?

2969. Can you recall a time when peer pressure hit you hardest—and how did you respond?

2970. If a tornado warning came through your area, what's your immediate response?

2971. What was your most recent train journey—and what do you remember about it?

2972. If you were naming a dynamic detective duo, what two names would sound cool together?

2973. What greenery or blooms would make your dream garden feel complete?

2974. What's your ideal steeping time for a perfect cup of tea—short and light, or long and bold?

2975. If you could choose any person, place, or idea to feature on a coin, what would it be?

2976. Do you tend to fall asleep the same way every night—or do you move around?

2977. What's the strangest app you've ever come across—either funny, creepy, or totally random?

2978. What moment recently brought up feelings of envy—and how did you handle it?

2979. If you could win unlimited access to anything for life, what would you choose?

2980. If you had 25 hours in a day instead of 24, how would you use the extra time?

2981. If teddy bears had their own feast, what would you imagine they serve each other?

2982. Have you ever accidentally damaged something in a store and had to own up to it?

2983. What's something you often stress over—even though others say it's no big deal?

2984. If you were a dog for a day, how many tennis balls do you think you could hold?

2985. What topic came up in conversation this week that really caught your interest?

2986. What film would become hilariously absurd if you added "versus zombles" to the title?

2987. Have you ever cracked the Rubik's Cube? How long did it take you the first time?

2988. What's something you recently needed to be forgiven for—and how did that go?

2989. If you had four babies at once, what names would you give them—any themes?

2990. If someone asked you to name one food that screams 'America,' what would it be?

2991. What's your most memorable seatmate story—someone odd, surprising, or unforgettable?

2992. In your experience, what topic sparks arguments more than any other?

2993. What word do you find yourself misspelling no matter how many times you try?

2994. If you were to design a truly unforgettable proposal, what would it look like?

2995. If you could invite three well-known people to join you for a game of Twister, who would they be?

2996. What interest, habit, or phase did you once think would last forever—but didn't?

2997. Do you ever get strong gut feelings or premonitions—and how do you describe that?

2998. When did someone's words or actions last catch you off guard in a hurtful way?

2999. When the sky is clear and the weather is just right, what outdoor activity calls to you?

3000. What common saying or bit of advice doesn't sit right with you— and why?

Enjoy a Free Digital Copy of This Transformational Journal—My Gift to You

Thank you for showing up for yourself and taking this powerful step toward daily self-care, reflection, and personal growth.

As a heartfelt gift, I'm offering you a FREE digital copy of THIS IS MY WAY: 365 Positive Thoughts and Self-Care Journal.

It's packed with inspiring messages and thought-provoking questions to help you build confidence, reduce anxiety, and reconnect with what matters most —all year long.

Claim your free e-copy by scanning this QR code:

Prefer a Physical Copy?

Many readers love having a physical copy to hold, highlight, or gift to someone special. If that sounds like you, you can grab your printed copy here:

Buy the hardcover version on Amazon by scanning this QR code:

Thank you for allowing me to be a small part of your self-care journey.

Here's to a year of reflection, growth, and positive change.

Aria Capri Publishing

www.ingramcontent.com/pod-product-compliance
Lightning Source LLC
Chambersburg PA
CBHW031500120626
46545CB00005B/1682